BRITTANY
AND NORMANDY

1 (frontispiece, overleaf): Pointe du Raz, the most westerly point of mainland Europe. On the horizon the Ile de Sein is just visible

Mary Elsy

BRITTANY
AND
NORMANDY

B. T. Batsford Ltd London

First published 1974
Copyright © Mary Elsy, 1974
ISBN 0 7134 2811 2

Printed and bound by Cox & Wyman Ltd
Fakenham, Norfolk
for the publishers, B. T. Batsford Ltd
4 Fitzhardinge Street, London W1H 0AH

Contents

Illustrations

Acknowledgements

The Author and Publisher would like to thank the following for the illustrations appearing in this book : Bavaria Verlag for no. 2; Anne Bolt for nos. 1 and 13; Pat Brindley for no. 19; Douglas Dickins for nos. 4, 15 and 16; the French General Tourist Office for no. 18; J. Allan Cash for no. 5; A. F. Kersting for nos. 3, 6, 7, 8, 9, 10, 11, 12, 14, 17, 20, 21, 22, 23, 24 and 25.

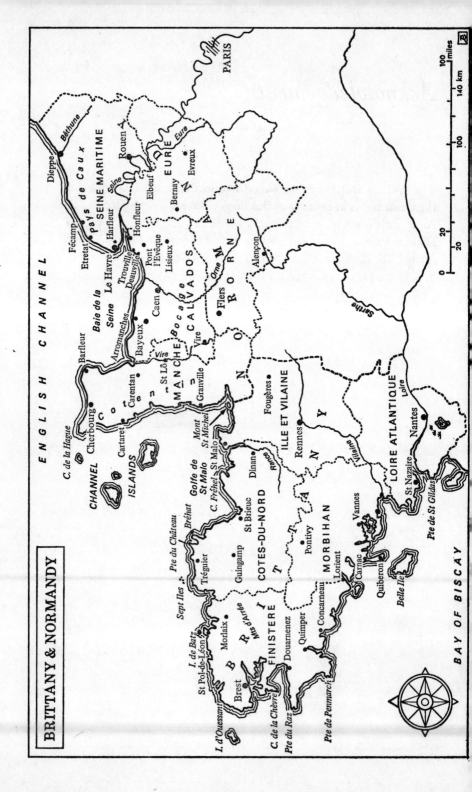

BRITTANY & NORMANDY

Part 1
Brittany

1. History and Introduction

Although it may seem strange to put two provinces so different as Normandy and Brittany into one book, they do have some things in common. The greater part of the two regions were once joined as Armorica and then, in Roman times, as Lugdensis Secunda. Both provinces had ties of blood and trade with Britain. Both (although Brittany to a lesser extent) were later used as a springboard for English invasions of France. Also the sea has played an important part in the lives of both provinces, helping to produce sailors, explorers, emigrants – and pirates. Finally, as part of France, their adjoining coastline forms one of the most popular areas in Europe with British holidaymakers.

While we owe so much of our early institutions to Normandy, Brittany, whose name means 'Little Britain', is part of our ancient history. Its quiet countryside is reminiscent of Devonshire, its craggy coast of Cornwall, while the barren moors in western Finistère (*finis terrae* – 'land's end') are similar to Scotland.

Brittany's history has been determined by its isolated position. This maritime land with the long head, the Brittany peninsula, pointing 180 miles out to sea, on one side the English Channel, on the other the Atlantic Ocean, was once cut off from the rest of France by forests and desolate moorlands.

Little is yet known about its earliest inhabitants, a Mediterranean people. Those in southern Brittany had a fairly prosperous trade in tin and copper, controlling the sea routes from northern Spain and the British Isles, and land routes along the Loire Valley towards the Seine and central Europe. They left behind their culture in the shape of megaliths – menhirs (long stones), dolmens (stone tables) and cromlechs (circles of standing stones), the most numerous and famous being those at Carnac in the Morbihan. Like those of Stonehenge, they were most probably connected in some way with the sun, but the definition of their exact purpose is still controversial.

The Celts, who arrived on the peninsula in the sixth century B.C. and who probably intermarried with the previous inhabitants, divided the land between five tribes. Interestingly enough, this division is very similar to the division of the province into five departments in 1794. The Redones occupied, roughly, Ille et Vilaine, having their centre at Rennes; the Namnetes inhabited Loire Atlantique (but since 1964 this is part of the Pays de la Loire and is no longer in Brittany officially); the Coriosolitae of the Côtes-du-Nord had their centre at Corseul (this is now an unimportant village): the Osismi occupied an area somewhat larger than the present Finistère and had their centre at Carhaix (now quite an important town), while the Veneti occupied Morbihan, with their centre near Vannes. These Celts, who introduced iron, built boats 30 metres long and based their livelihood on the sea.

The Veneti, especially, were particularly fine sailors, as Julius Caesar found to his cost when he tried to make Brittany part of his Roman Gaul. That he succeeded was due chiefly to guile and good luck rather than to superior seamanship. In 56 B.C., one year before his invasion of Britain, a famous sea battle took place near Port Navalo, off the southern coast. The wind dropped, becalming the Veneti in their sailing ships, but favouring the Romans in their oar-propelled galleys. The Romans tied sickles to ropes. Whenever one of their boats drew alongside an enemy sailing ship, a sailor heaved it into the rigging. Then the galley swept on. As the rope was dragged tight, so down came the rigging and sail. The sailing ship was then attacked and boarded. This sea victory over the powerful Veneti, who were most barbarously treated, enabled Caesar to subjugate the rest of Brittany.

Even so, this impenetrable peninsula was only superficially Romanized, as was its later Christianization. The Celts used the menhirs they found in their own religion, as did the earliest Romans, who carved pictures of their gods on some of them. Brittany was still predominantly a pagan province when the Romans left in the fifth century A.D.

The next wave of invasion, which took place during the fifth and sixth centuries, was a peaceful one. It was of fellow Celts from Britain across the water. Whether they were driven out by Anglo-Saxons settling there, or whether they were merely emigrating has not yet been properly researched. But these new colonists, chiefly farmers, gave Armor (land of the sea) its present name Brittany. With them came Celtic missionaries, especially from Ireland and Wales, who completed the provinces' conversion to Christianity. They sanctified many of the pagan menhirs by crowning them with a cross, and divided the country into large parishes – forerunners of today's communes. Many of them were made saints by the Bretons who named towns and villages after them: St Malo, St Brieuc, St Pol-de-Léon are a few.

Under Charlemagne Brittany became an outpost of the Frankish empire and was divided into petty lordships. Its colonization, as under the Romans, was only a superficial one. One Carolingian emperor, Louis the Pious, gave Nominoé, Count of Vannes, the job of keeping the Bretons under control in A.D. 826 in the hope that they would be more likely to obey one of their own kind. Nominoé did quell a riot in 836, but would not allow Frankish troops into Brittany. Later, when Louis died and fighting broke out among his sons, Nominoé promised loyalty to the one called Charles the Bold and even supplied him with soldiers up to 842. This squabbling amongst the brothers enabled him to strengthen his own position and declare his independence. In 845 he managed to throw off the Frankish domination in a battle near Redon. An old stone cross and a modern statue of Nominoé, father of Brittany, stand near the site, now a hamlet called La Bataille. Nominoé died on 7 March 851, near Vendôme, but his independent dynasty was to last for more than a century.

Norman invasions of Brittany took place in the tenth century. In 937, the young Alain Barbe Torte ('crooked beard'), heir to the

Breton crown, returned to Brittany from his sanctuary at the English court of King Athelstan, and rallied the people. Many of these pirates were slaughtered on the Loire below Nantes. The rest were driven out of the country. Alain rebuilt Nantes and made it the capital of the duchy. However, in spite of the victory the battle with the Norsemen had weakened his dynasty, enabling the Breton nobles to defy his successors. Internal strife and poverty were to last until the end of the fourteenth century.

Brittany continued to have many contacts with England across the sea. One duke, Alan the Red, who accompanied William the Conqueror to England in 1066, was later granted Yorkshire lands, formerly belonging to Edwin Earl of Mercia, where he built Richmond Castle. Another duke, Alan III, the first duke to be formally styled Earl of Richmond, fought beside King Stephen at the battle of Lincoln in 1141. Yet another, John I, fought for Edward I in the Welsh wars in 1277.

Brittany remained fiercely jealous of her independence; France's kings had to wait a long time before they could make themselves felt there. By the Treaty of Gisors in 1113, Louis VI had to abandon direct overlordship of Brittany to Henry I of England, also Duke of Normandy. Later, the marriage of Henry II's son Geoffrey to Constance, daughter of Count Conan of Brittany, brought the province even further into England's orbit.

However, Philippe Auguste showed himself to be an astute statesman as well as king. He put himself in the rôle of Brittany's protector by taking the part of Constance and her son Arthur when Arthur claimed the throne of England in succession to his uncle, Richard I. He later abandoned Arthur at the peace of Le Goulet on 2 May 1200, by which Arthur was left only in possession of Brittany, which he held as a fief to his uncle John. But Philippe was only biding his time. Two years later John was disinherited by the French royal court. The seizure of most of his French possessions enabled the king to confer Brittany on Arthur as a royal fief. The Treaty of Gisors was set aside and Brittany returned to France's royal overlordship.

The unfortunate Arthur, a mere sixteen-year-old pawn in the

2   *The calvary at Guimiliau, near Morlaix*

3   St Thégonnec, Finistère

royal game, was later captured by John at Mirebeau, and eventually murdered, probably at Rouen castle, by his uncle John. The heiress was his sister, Eleanor, then living at Bristol and the ward of King John, who, as her guardian, claimed the right to administer her inheritance. This, of course, would have delivered the province into the hands of the king of England, just as undesirable to the Bretons as being in the hands of the French king. So her claim was set on one side by an assembly of Breton lords and prelates at Vannes in 1203. Her half-sister, Alix (daughter of Constance and her third husband, Guy of Thouars) was set in her place. Her father, Guy, was made ward of the fief. Later, because Guy was proved to have been involved in pro-English intrigues, Philippe had the excuse to take the governorship of Brittany into his own hands.

Alix was married to a member of the French royal family, Peter of Dreux (grandson of Louis VI), usually known as Peter Mauclerc. However, although Peter did liege honour to Louis VIII for Brittany in 1213, during the regency that followed this king's death he also became involved in rebellious feudal coalitions, and even did homage to Henry III of England in 1229, supporting him against the French king. But his ambitions came to nothing and when his son, John I (the Red), came of age, he relinquished the governorship of Brittany to him.

John I (1237–86), John II (1286–1305), Arthur II (1305–12) and John III (1312–41) were all obedient vassals to the French crown, yet were sufficiently adroit to retain the honour (territory) of Richmond. In 1297, the French king, Philip the Fair, conferred the rank of duke on John II and admitted him to the peerage of France. Their loyalty, however, enabled the French king to intervene freely in Brittany, which he could treat like a royal domain, and obtain services in men and money when needed.

This line of French dukes, ruling from Rennes, ended on the death of the childless John III in 1341. The resulting war over who was to succeed him brought England and France into open conflict again.

The contestants were Charles of Blois (1319–64), married to

John III's niece, Jeanne de Penthièvre, who was supported by the French, and John of Montfort, John III's brother, who was supported by the English Edward III.

The matter was finally resolved in 1364 at the battle of Auray when Charles of Blois, although backed by the great Breton military leader, Du Guesclin, was defeated and killed, and John of Montfort's son (John of Montfort himself now being dead) became John IV. A peace was signed in Guérande in 1365. Charles of Blois, incidentally, was regarded as a saint by the Bretons and a cult grew up round his grave and relics at Grâces, near Guincamp.

This war of succession had brought Brittany to near ruin and the de Montfort dukes (John IV, V and Peter II) tried to secure her neutrality during the rest of the Hundred Years' War (1337–1453). These dukes governed the province from Nantes almost as an independent country, paying homage, but only in theory, to the king of France. They proved good rulers, restoring the ravaged duchy, which then entered into one of the most brilliant periods of her history.

François II, duke of Brittany from 1458 to 1488, continued this policy of maintaining Breton independence against any encroachments by the French king, even if it meant relying on foreign support. He allied himself with England and made a treaty with Edward IV, whereby his eldest daughter, Anne, should marry the Prince of Wales.

The future of the Duchy was dependent on her marriage; many rival claimants sought her hand. Anne herself favoured Maximilian of Austria, whom she married by proxy. But, unfortunately for her, his own country's affairs prevented him from defending his bride.

In 1488 the Bretons, who had supported a federal coalition against the regent of France, Anne of Beaujeu, were defeated at St Aubin du Cormier. François was obliged to sign the Treaty of Verger in which he undertook only to contract marriage for his daughters, Anne and Isabelle, with the French king's permission. François died a few weeks later, it is said of a broken heart.

4 *Pont-Aven, near Quimperlé*

A few years later, in 1491, the youthful Anne was besieged at Rennes by Charles VIII, whose terms included the rupture of her marriage with Maximilian and her marriage with himself. Anne had little option but to agree. Also, by the terms of her marriage, if he died without issue, she would have to marry his successor. And this is what happened! The ugly, rather stupid Charles died in 1498, and Anne was then obliged to marry the prematurely aged Duke of Orléans, the next king, Louis XII. He in turn had to divorce his first wife.

Anne, who died in 1514, has always held a very high place in Breton history. She was a devout Catholic and a patroness of the arts. She also devoted herself to the administration of the duchy, jealously guarding its autonomy. She tried to arrange a marriage between her daughter Claude (by Louis) with Maximilian's grandson, Charles, but eventually had to agree to her betrothal with François d'Angoulême, the future François I.

Shortly after Claude's marriage in 1515, the young duchess found herself Queen of France. She was persuaded to yield her duchy to their son, the Dauphin. Claude died in 1524 and in 1532, the States (Council) meeting at Vannes proclaimed the perpetual union of the county and duchy of Brittany with the kingdom and crown of France. So, at long last, Brittany was united with France. Even so, the duchy retained many of its rights and privileges and its provincial autonomy was to survive until the French Revolution.

The mass of the Bretons, staunchly Catholic, were not much affected by the ideas of the Reformation. Even so, the country was the scene of much fighting. Bandits, such as the notorious La Fontenelle, were able to flourish unchecked. In 1588, the duc de Mercoeur, a governor of Brittany, took advantage of the anarchic situation to lead a resistance against the Protestant French king, Henri IV. Spain sent 7,000 Spanish troops to help his cause. He set up a parliament at Nantes and even put forward his son Philip to be duke of Brittany.

Mercoeur won a victory at Craun in Anjou in 1592, but lost ground when Henri IV was 'converted' to Catholicism (you will probably remember his 'Paris is worth a Mass'). The Bretons, worn out with Mercoeur's ambitions and their country's disorder, sent a pressing appeal to the King to come and restore peace. Mercoeur finally resigned Brittany in 1598. Henri IV put an end to religious strife – for the time anyway – by the Edict of Nantes, signed 13 August 1598, at the great castle of the Dukes overlooking the Loire.

The seventeenth century was a time of prosperity. Brittany, emerging at last from isolation and conflict, benefited from her union with France. Sixty towns were created, trade developed, especially fishing, textiles and printing. Castles and châteaux were built and enlarged. The ports of St Malo, Lorient and Nantes were expanded. Brittany, organized politically as a French province, did sometimes come in conflict with the crown. The Stamped Paper Act of 1675 (the minister, Colbert, decreed that all legal acts should be recorded on stamped paper) led to an indignant uprising, but this was put down.

At first, many Bretons welcomed the Revolution, but soon became disgusted by its excesses, especially the execution of the King and the notorious drownings of royalists at Nantes in October 1793. The new republic also tampered with their autonomy and privileges, persecuted their priests, and tried to enforce conscription. Many rose against it, joining the *chouans*, a name given to bands of peasants, also smugglers and dealers in contraband salt, who added their support to the rebellious Vendéean royalists. *Chouan* means 'screech owl' in Breton for the chouans were also night birds who used the hoot of an owl as a signal.

Chouanism was finally put down after the defeat of the royalist exiles landing at Quiberon Bay in 1795. The wild countryside in which they hid was cleared. Even so, chouanism still smoulders on, but now in the form of Breton nationalism.

The construction of roads, railways and canals over the last hundred years have helped to bring this individualistic province more in line with the rest of France. Brittany lost many soldiers and sailors in the First World War. In the Second, she contributed the largest number of men in France to the Free French Forces and the Resistance movement. Some of the fiercest battles that followed the allied landings in 1944 took place in Brittany – Lorient, Brest, St Nazaire and St Malo were all badly damaged in the fighting.

Since 1945, thanks to the Common Market, Brittany has become more outward-looking. Even so it is still a relatively undeveloped province with poor communications when compared with the rest of France. Although the birth-rate is high, the country is under-occupied because so many Bretons emigrate to work in Paris.

Industrialization has considerably advanced since the Fifth Plan (1961–70) as the zone qualifies for the highest amount of assistance. Some of today's important industries are shipbuilding, building and civil engineering, electronics and electrical engineering (fairly recently introduced), mining and quarrying, fish, fruit and vegetable canning and motor manufacturing (Citroën has two large factories at Rennes). Then there is the thermal power station run on fuel oil at Brest, a nuclear power station at Mont d'Arrée and the 540,000,000 LWH tidal power station on the river Rance, near Dinard. There are also smaller industries, such as textiles, shoe manufacturing, tanning and papermaking, as well as numerous local crafts.

About 30 per cent of the population still live by farming (more than 60 per cent of the land surface is under cultivation), but many of the holdings are too small, although thanks to organizations such as SAFER and FASASA they are gradually being merged into larger units. Brittany's soil is very varied, ranging from scrubby moorland to rich soil. Much market gardening (especially of leaf artichokes and cauliflowers) takes place along the sheltered parts of the coast, where the climate is influenced by the Gulf Stream, and around the Loire. There are many apple orchards, especially for cider apples, and stock-raising farms (particularly cows and pigs). Brittany is France's leading milk producer. Much of the agricultural and dairy produce is sold abroad or in other parts of France.

The Bretons still have many similarities with the Cornish and Irish and especially the Welsh people. About one million of her approximately three million inhabitants, who live chiefly in the western half, speak or understand Breton, which is very like Welsh. Although Breton is not taught in the schools, Rennes University does have a chair of Celtic studies and there are regular broadcasts in Breton on the regional ORTF network.

However, Breton has never been an official language, even during the days of the province's independence. From about the eleventh century onwards, upper-class Bretons wrote first in Latin, then in French. Since the Middle Ages works in Breton have been mainly translations from Latin or French, or fifteenth-century mystery plays. There was a revival of interest in the nineteenth century when many poems and ballads were written in Breton. But although Brittany has produced many writers, some as renowned as Chateaubriand, Ernest Renan and Jules Verne, they usually chose to write in French.

The Bretons are an imaginative people with a love of the fantastic, the eerie and the supernatural. The province is well-named the land of legends, the home of magicians, fairies, demons and saints. Especially saints. Each town, village and hamlet can claim its own saint, usually made without any reference to the Pope or Roman Catholic church. It is said that there are more saints in Brittany than there are stones in the ground.

The sea has played, and still does, a large part in many of the people's lives. Most of France's sailors and fishermen come from Brittany. There are innumerable fishing villages, strung out all along the rugged rocky coast. The seafood gathered – oysters, tunny, mackerel, lobsters, prawns, shrimps, sardines, to mention a few – make it a fish-lover's paradise. In the past, especially, the price paid was a high one : the sea claimed many victims.

So the Bretons have a great respect for the sea. Every year the boats are blessed. Priests lead processions which wade through the waters to the fishing boats and their nets; they pray for a good catch and a safe return for their crew from all their expeditions.

The Bretons, especially those from western Brittany, are a deeply religious people. Mystical and joyous festivals, called Pardons, are held all over Brittany in honour of the saints of a particular chapel or church. The name comes from the churches' custom of granting indulgences to pardon people's sins on a Saint's Day. There is often a legend woven round the Pardon of many of these places.

The Pardon starts with a mass. Then comes an open-air service when people pray before an altar of the saint in whose honour the festival is being held. A procession of priests and villagers chanting and singing, carrying candles and banners and a shrine of the saint, winds through the streets. The traditional costume of the region is worn on these occasions, especially by the women. Very often the Pardon ends with a fair. You would probably see dancing to bagpipes and wrestling, a traditional Breton sport.

Because of poverty and long periods of internal strife, Brittany has far fewer fine cathedrals and churches than Normandy. Only a few small churches were built during the Romanesque period of the eleventh and twelfth centuries. Also the style of building was much influenced by the use of local granite, which is a hard and difficult stone to work with. The construction of large churches and cathedrals was usually held up by financial difficulties, with the result that they tend to incorporate the architectural features of many centuries. Examples of this are to be seen at St Pol de Léon, Tréguier, Quimper, Nantes and Dol.

Except on the eastern border and along the coast, there are few great castles in Brittany. Kerjean, Josselin and the ducal castle at Nantes are three half palace-fortresses. With the exceptions of the ruling dukes and a few great families, most of the Breton nobility were poor and lived in simple manor farms.

Art in Brittany reached its highest expression in religion, especially in the size and decoration of the parish churches. From the fifteenth to the eighteenth centuries Breton sculptors, usually local men, worked in wood and stone to decorate church interiors. Rood screens, baptismal fonts and pulpits are particularly finely done in many Breton churches, as are many of the stained glass windows and pieces of gold plate.

The parish closes, mostly built during the seventeenth century, are a typical Breton feature. There was a tremendous rivalry between neighbouring villages about the grandeur of their closes.

The cemetery, which is often reached by a triumphal arch, is surrounded by the church, the calvary and ossuary. The calvary, a tall decorated structure, most probably a descendant of the menhir, which later gave way to the cross, was used for religious teaching by the priests. As its name implies, these monuments are carved to depict the Passion of our Lord, the events leading up to the crucifixion and the events that succeeded it. Jesus on the cross is usually the focal point and around him are gathered the persons who took part in this great drama, such as the apostles, the Virgin Mary, angels and archangels.

But Brittany's greatest attraction for tourists is its 3,500 km. of jagged coastline, tall cliffs and wide sandy beaches. The shore and the fertile land behind is still known as the Armor (land of the sea), while the interior, also attractive, with its wooded hills, moorlands, cultivated fields and pastures is still the Argoat (land of the forest: because so much of it was once covered in trees).

Brittany's climate – mild, humid, windy and variable – could be called oceanic. There are differences, although not very great, within the regions. The north is colder than the south, which is warmed by the arrival of waters from the tropical areas of the Atlantic into the Gulf of Gascony. Mediterranean plants, such as palm trees, mimosas and magnolias flourish along the southern shores, as they do along the part of the north coast influenced by the Gulf Stream. The climate also grows colder as one moves eastwards. Brest is a few degrees warmer than Rennes. It is also wetter. But although Brittany has the reputation of being a rather wet province, its annual rainfall is lower than in many other parts of France. This is because its rain, although fairly frequent, is also fine.

Brittany, which represents about five per cent of France, divides roughly into two areas, higher Brittany in the east, and lower Brittany in the west. These names are odd in that higher Brittany is low, while lower Brittany is hilly. Millions of years ago higher Brittany was covered by a shallow sea, while lower Brittany was an island. Today even the highest hills in the west do not reach 400 metres. The highest in the Monts d'Arrée is 385 metres, in the

Montagnes Noires 326 metres, while the Menez Hom is 330 metres.

When France was divided into 21 regions in 1964 Brittany, as a peninsula lying between two seas, with all its customs and historical traditions, was the one with the greatest geographical unity and homogeneity. Except that the department, the Loire Inférieure, later called the Loire Atlantique, has now been controversially incorporated into the Pays de la Loire, its divisions are much the same as they were before the Romans arrived. Because of this, I have divided the book into the departments, Ille et Vilaine (capital Rennes), Côtes-du-Nord (capital St Brieuc), Finistère (capitals Morlaix, Brest and Quimper), Morbihan (capital Vannes), still throwing the traditional Loire Atlantique (capital, Nantes) in for good measure, and moving in an anti-clockwise direction round the province.

2. Ille et Vilaine

Rennes and its surroundings

Rennes, capital of the department, Ille et Vilaine, and Brittany's major city, is also the province's front door to France, the main entrance to the western peninsula. Strategically situated at the junction of the Ille and Vilaine rivers in stockfarming and agricultural country, it is also a commercial and industrial centre, possesses an important university, and is the seat of an archbishopric. It has expanded considerably over the last half century: in 1936 it had a population of 98,000; in 1976 this will be 200,000.

Rennes, centre of the Celtic Redones, was the commercial centre of Armorica under the Romans, who surrounded it with a wall. It became the seat of the dukes of Brittany in the tenth century. After the union of upper and lower Brittany it was proclaimed capital in 1213 and the dukes came here to claim their crowns. The *Parlement* of Brittany was held here from 1561 to 1675 when, because of the uprising against the unpopular stamp act, it was transferred to Vannes until 1689. The Rennes *Parlement* opposed the *ancien régime* on several occasions, as also it did the decrees of the Constituent Assembly of the French Revolution. It later became reconciled with the Revolution and Rennes was the headquarters of the Republican army during their fight against the army of the Vendée.

In spite of its age and although its history is closely bound up with Brittany, Rennes, stately, cultured, coldly classical, appears more French than Breton.

The reason for this is that on 22 December 1720 a great fire, which lasted a week, swept through its old medieval buildings, destroying much of the town. The story goes that a drunken carpenter set fire to a heap of shavings with his lamp. As there was no running water or proper way of putting out a fire in those days, and with the wind acting like a bellows, the blaze grew worse. About a thousand buildings were destroyed.

Because of this catastrophe much of the town had to be rebuilt, mostly at the crown's expense. The two architects, Jacques Gabriel and his son, Jacques-Anges (he was also responsible for the Place de la Concorde in Paris) had it built *à la* Louis xv, quite an innovation at that time – very uniform, with tall houses set in wide rectangular streets.

Even so, there is still a little bit of old Rennes with its maze of cobbled street, fifteenth- and sixteenth-century gabled houses and superior eighteenth-century *maisons* with sculptured façades for you to see. One tourist speciality is the pancake shop (pancakes are particularly popular in Brittany), 22 Rue du Chapitre. Near by is the eighteenth-century Hôtel de Blossac, which has a particularly fine staircase. The house called Ti Koz, which is supposed to have belonged to Du Guesclin, is now an attractive and expensive pancake restaurant.

The 'kings' and 'queens' of Brittany rode through the old gate, the Porte Mordelaise, which is fortified by two towers, to the cathedral. They entered the town by this route when travelling in special processions to be crowned in the cathedral.

Rennes cathedral is dedicated to St Pierre and is the third to be built on this site since the sixth century. The present one was finished in 1844, after 57 years' work. But its façade, granite and imposing, dates from 1540 to 1703. The interior, a mixture of Roman Byzantine and Renaissance styles, seems rather dark, but has a mellow atmosphere and beautiful ceiling. Pink granite pillars blend well with the mauve of the stained-glass windows. The organ is worth looking at, as is the high altar, decorated by Flemish craftsmen showing scenes from the life of the Virgin Mary, in a chapel at the rear. For interest, look at the statue of the bishop of Rennes who died in A.D. 505 : it is dressed in robes and lies inside an ornate *châsse* in the chapel of St Amand. Whenever there was a calamity threatening the town this holy man's statue was carried through the town in the hope that he would use his influence with the powers above.

But the imposing Palais de Justice, overlooking the Place du Palais, is Rennes' most famous building. You enter first the Salle des Gros Piliers, a large vestibule with rather austere columns, where it is not too difficult to imagine markets being held. The fine double staircase leads to the first floor and city hall (1734), empty, unused and still a little shabby. But all around it lie a number of magnificent rooms, decorated by painters such as Jouvenel and Coypel.

The most impressive of them is the Grande Chambre, Rennes' parliamentary debating chamber. Sixty feet long, 30 feet wide and 22 feet high, it has particularly beautiful panelling, paintings, gilded woodwork and ceiling. Tapestries on the wall show important events in Brittany's history, such as the marriage of the Duchess Anne and Charles viii of France. Although the originals were destroyed during the French Revolution, these modern Gobelins, which took 24 years to make (one person doing one metre a year), are priceless. A box overlooking the chamber was used sometimes by Madame de Sévigné, who took a great interest in the proceedings.

The Palais was also the supreme court of 2,300 Breton tribunals and so played an important legislative as well as political rôle. Most of the counsellors and presidents were chosen from the noble families of the province. Members of the Rennes *Parlement* were much respected and traditionally had large families. A seat could be bought for something like £21,000 in today's terms. Salaries for court officials were low, but judges received 'spice' (this was chiefly sweets and preserves) from their clients. Today all the Palais is used for law courts.

When in Rennes you should visit the Thabor Gardens, reckoned to be the second-best flower garden of France. It shows a variety of garden arrangements, such as a formal French garden growing flowers from all regions, a skilfully designed landscape one, an attractive rose garden, also a botanical one. For children there is a miniature zoo with monkeys, guinea pigs, parrots and other birds, set around a pagoda. The whole park covers an area of about 25 acres, and its nucleus once belonged to the Benedictine Abbey of St Melaine (Melaine, a famous bishop, was also a great healer and adviser to Clovis). The church is worth a visit.

Rennes' Musée de Bretagne is worth seeing, too, as it shows the history of the province and has some good examples of Breton furniture, kitchen utensils (those most enormous pans must have fed giants), and most interesting of all, a collection of the colourful costumes of the region.

Rennes is an excellent centre for tours by rail, bus or car. On its east side lie the border castle towns, such as Vitré, Fougères and Combourg.

Walled Vitré, situated on a spur overlooking the Vilaine valley, with its impressive castle perched watchfully high above, has preserved its medieval character. Its heyday was from the sixteenth to the eighteenth centuries when it was renowned for its textiles, woollen cloth and cotton stockings. Today, although it still has factories, it acts chiefly as a market for farm produce.

The best view of the town is from the castle watch path. English visitors will be interested to know that the suburb of Rachapt was occupied by their compatriots for several years during the Hundred Years' War, while they were besieging the castle and town. Eventually the frustrated inhabitants paid them to go away. So when you cross this area, whose name translates into 'repurchase', you will know how it got it. The museum, installed in three of the castle's towers, is worth seeing.

The Château des Rochers, home of Madame de Sévigné, whose lively letters tell much about country life and Vitré during the time of Louis XIV, is not far from here. Les Rochers is still owned by members of her family, but you can see the chapel and her own room, known as the Green Room, which is filled with her possessions. The garden beyond was laid out by Le Nôtre.

Also near by is the village of Champeaux with its charming square and attractive fourteenth- and fifteenth-century church.

Fougères, set beside a forest (3,900 acres of trees) about 46 km. to the north-east of Rennes, stands at the intersection of the main roads linking Brittany with Paris and the Channel ports. So you are likely to pass through it if you come into Brittany via Normandy.

Like Vitré, it is set picturesquely on a promontory overlooking a valley, the Nançon, but its castle, one of the most famous in France, is situated below, almost surrounded by water. It has a history as romantic as its appearance. Victor Hugo introduced Fougères into *Quatre-Vingt-Treize* and Balzac put it into *Les Chouans*. Both authors obtained their copy by visiting the castle. Balzac even talked to survivors of the rebellion.

However, in spite of its hugeness – 13 towers connected by ramparts – the castle has often been captured. Henry II of England, Pierre Mauclerc (not for long though), Du Guesclin, Charles VIII, Mercoeur, the Vendéeans, are just a few who have held it.

Fougères the town has been more successful than its castle and Vitré. It switched from manufacturing sailcloth to ladies' shoes, for which it is particularly famous, readymade clothes, lingerie and other light industries. But because of its greater industrialization there is less of interest to see. The best way to spend an afternoon there is to walk round the castle's outer fortifications and have a guided tour of its interior.

The castle at Combourg, rising above a little old town set beside a lake, looks like a theatrical set-piece, which is as it should be since it was the home for a period of Du Guesclin, Brittany's most famous military leader, and also of Chateaubriand, her greatest writer. Built in the eleventh century, it was enlarged in the fourteenth and fifteenth centuries.

Chateaubriand, born at St Malo, had a chequered and up-and-down career. He fought for the royalists at Valmy, then escaped to England, where he lived in great poverty. During the Restoration his fortunes rose again, when he became France's ambassador to England. He spent two years at Combourg as an impressionable and dreamy child, so perhaps its gloomy atmosphere and the then rather desolate surroundings of woodland and heath helped to mould his later mystical style. He slept high up in a turret called the Tour de Chat (Cat's Tower), because it was supposed to be haunted by a former Lord of Combourg, who returned each night in the form of a cat. You can visit his room, which has been turned into a museum and from which there is a good view of the surrounding countryside.

About 37 km. west of Rennes lies the Paimpont forest, covering an area of about 40 sq. km., and part of the eastern remains of Brittany's Argoat. Here still grow the old ashes and beeches, also firs and pines, although many of these have been fairly recently replanted to counteract the spread of broom and gorse scrubland.

This is King Arthur country, where this legendary king is supposed to have lived with his knights, ladies, hermits, magicians, not forgetting the Korrigan (the Breton leprechaun), and to have sought the Holy Grail.

It is a region of lakes and legends. A stone from the fountain of Baronton could unleash a wild storm, while the fairy, Vivianne, who captured the wizard Merlin in a magic circle, was born in the now empty château of Comper. Morgane, Arthur's sister, and a pupil of Merlin, ruled over the picturesque Val sans Retour, where she is supposed to have captured, imprisoned and punished people, especially naughty boys. Only the bold Sir Launcelot could deliver them from her witchery.

The village of Paimpont, set beside a pool and surrounded by trees, only dates from the Revolution. A seventh-century monastery, then a twelfth-century abbey once stood here. But of all this only the thirteenth-century church remains.

Sleepy Dol, lying to the north of Rennes, can quickly be reached by train. It is also situated on the tourist route between Mont St Michel and St Malo.

Old timbered houses and the most interesting part of the town lie along the Grand' Rue des Stuarts. Steep side turnings on the right lead up to its old cathedral, St Samson, a curious structure, a large sprawling mixture of centuries, with towers and turrets somehow putting one in mind of a Norman fortress.

Dol has no right to a cathedral as it is no longer a bishopric.

That it ever was one is due to the fact that until some time between the fifth and eighth centuries the marshland and Bay of St Michel were covered by a great forest. St Michel and Dol stood on hills but became islands when the sea flooded over this area. When the waters fell, leaving marshes, they were not drained until about the twelfth century onwards. But by then there were bishoprics at both St Malo and Dol although they were only about 24 km. apart.

Dol, lying on the frontier between Normandy and Brittany, was often besieged by the Normans. In 1076 William the Conqueror was defeated by this proud little town. In 1203, John, murderer of Prince Arthur, took Dol, burned its Romanesque cathedral, and occupied the town for a year. Later, perhaps overcome by remorse, he sent funds for the construction of the present cathedral, which dates from the thirteenth century. Altogether about 80 bishops have occupied the see of Dol. The first was St Samson in the sixth or seventh century; the last was M. Hercé, who distinguished himself by being shot along with other royalist supporters at Vannes in 1795 after the failure of the Quiberon invasion.

Inside the cathedral there is still much to remind one of its bishops. Unfortunately, when I visited it, it was undergoing repairs: some things were missing and it was not at its best. The interior is long, cool and grey with a particularly fine stained-glass medallion window in the chancel. The 80 fourteenth-century stalls are fascinating. Each arm-rest has a face carved on it, of nuns, monks and some which look suspiciously like devils.

Behind the cathedral lies the Promenade des Douves, a pleasant place to picnic and enjoy a good view of the Marais, the drained salty marshland, now a fertile area and renowned for its mutton, which stretches rather monotonously towards the coast. You can also see Mont Dol, a 200-foot granite mound, from which many prehistoric animals and flint implements have been excavated.

According to legend, the devil and the archangel Michael were once engaged in mortal combat here. You can even see the marks made by the devil's bottom and his claws. It seems that the devil was worsted because he was thrown injured into the Trou du Diable. Even so, he did somehow manage to appear mockingly on

Mont St Michel, about 19 km. away. But the archangel leapt after him, giving a mighty spring and leaving his footprint for ever on the mount. The mystery, of course, is where did the devil go next?

The Chapel of Notre Dame de l'Espérance on Mont Dol, which replaced a signal tower put there in 1802, is today the centre of a popular pilgrimage.

On the other side of Dol is the Champ Dolent, which boasts a 63-metre menhir, one of the finest in Brittany. Its name means 'field of pain' and refers to a legendary struggle which took place there.

St Malo, its surroundings and the Emerald Coast

One's first view of St Malo, Brittany's sea gateway, should be from the deck of a ship in early morning, when the old walled city of the corsairs, so strategically placed on its small peninsula, slowly slides itself out like a hazy mirage from its place between sea and sky.

Perhaps the most remarkable thing about this ghostly image that gradually takes flesh is that it really no longer exists. St Malo died during a two-week siege in 1944 when it was pounded to death by the American forces in Cherbourg. What you see now is merely a restoration. The pinkish granite towers, turrets, houses and twisting cobbled streets, even the twelfth- to seventeenth-century cathedral of St Vincent, have all been painstakingly put back.

St Malo was named after a sixth-century priest from Wales, who settled in the Gallo-Roman town of Aleth (now St Servan), situated beside the Rance, behind the island peninsula. He converted the inhabitants to Christianity and became their first bishop. However, later Norman invasions forced the people to settle on the more easily defended rock to their north. The bishopric was transferred there in 1144, and strong ramparts were built round the town. Because of its impregnable position, it was able to develop along its own independent line, under the loose control of the church. Its motto is '*Ni Français, Ni Bretons, Malouins suis*', adopted between 1590 and 1594, during the wars of religion, when its inhabitants even managed to establish a republic.

St Malo became renowned for its traders, its seamen and its pirates. For its size it has produced quite a number of eminent men, such as Jacques Cartier, who discovered the mouth of the St Lawrence river and Canada; Duguay Trouin (1673–1736) and Surcouf (1773–1827) privateers who inflicted very heavy losses on the English, Dutch and Spanish fleets; not forgetting Chateaubriand, who was born here, the tenth and last child of a St Malo shipowner.

St Malo's best feature is still its oldest – the ramparts. Tides here are very high, and waves sometimes rise to as much as 40 feet. The battering-ram effect of the sea is tremendous and vibrations can be felt miles away. No wonder that the old walls, which have stood up to centuries of bashing, managed to survive the destruction of the town.

A walk round the ramparts, starting from the St Vincent gateway, takes about an hour, and gives you magnificent views of the bay. You will see the islands – Fort National (built by Vauban in 1689), the Ile du Grand Bé (this isolated spot, which contains the tomb of Chateaubriand, can be walked to at low tide) and the Petit Bé Isles. There is also a grand view of the Emerald Coast to the west of Dinard across the Rance river.

After passing the Grande Porte you will have a good view of the narrow isthmus, which joins the walled city to its suburbs, the harbours and St Servan. The ramparts, which skirt the houses of the rich St Malo shipowners, pass numerous little stairways and ramps from which you can descend to the town again if you wish. There are also many little parks with seats where you can rest and look out to sea.

Near St Thomas's gateway is the aquarium, which is built into the walls of the ramparts in the Place Vauban and which contains fish found around this part of the coast.

By now, you are near the Place Chateaubriand, the main part of St Malo, and close to its famous waxworks museum (Quic en

6   *Château de Combourg, childhood home of Chateaubriand*

Groigne), where you can see carefully reconstructed scenes from the history of St Malo. The words *'Quic en Groigne'* come from an inscription the sparky Duchess Anne had carved on the tower during a dispute with the Bishop of St Malo : *'Qui-qu'en groigne, ainsi sera, car tel est mon bon plaisir'*, meaning 'Whoever may complain of it, it shall be so, for such is my pleasure'.

St Malo's museum is situated in part of the castle. There are guided tours in English during the season, but it is useful if you can read French.

The first gallery shows the three aspects of the Malouins, as traders, as pirates, and as explorers. Their exploits were particularly terrific during the seventeenth century. They did not cease their war against England until 1815 and were not finished finally as privateers until 8 July 1856. The corsairs' weapons – pistols, daggers and swords – are shown along with some of their loot, such as captured coffers. One great prize was a bell taken from the English frigate *Hercules* in 1777.

An interesting model shows St Malo at the time of Jacques Cartier. Its ramparts were pierced by two gates, Grande Porte and St Thomas, and enclose the manor, cathedral, houses, cemeteries and fields.

The cathedral, St Vincent, has only recently been reconstructed. Dignified, spacious and Gothic, it blends old with new, being somehow modern yet old at the same time. The stained-glass windows, designed by Max Ingrand, are particularly fine. The cool grey interior is constantly warmed by shafts of yellow-mauve sunlight filtering through. There are a few old statues to be seen, but many empty niches are still waiting to be filled. Unfortunately the descending steps are not easy to see, and notices have been set up to warn the unwary to look where they're going.

Jacques Cartier's black slab tomb is very simple. He is also remembered by stones marking the spot where he stood in the cathedral on 17 May 1535 to receive the benediction of the Bishop of St Malo prior to his departure for the New World.

Apart from its quaintness and history, St Malo, which joins up with busy St Servan (which faces the Rance river and has shingle

7 *The beach at St Briac, Côtes-du-Nord*

beaches) and the spa resort Paramé (good beach), is a yachting centre, has a casino, and is particularly renowned for its seafood. It also makes a good centre for expeditions, both by land and sea.

Rothéneuf, a few miles farther to the east, within easy reach by bus, has picturesque pines, dunes, cliffs and good beaches and is a pleasant place for a family holiday. Cancale, farther on, is a picturesque fishing port and seaside resort (shingle beach). If you go there by car you should drive via the Pointe du Grouin, a wild rocky headland, from which there is a good view of the coast from Cap Fréhel to Mont St Michel.

The local bus to Cancale deposits you beside St Méen, its main church. Not far from the inside door is a book whose pages turn automatically after you have inserted a franc, and give information in three languages about the area. There is also a sailors' chapel dedicated to the 508 local men who were drowned at sea between 1846 and 1967.

If you descend the hill via the Rue de Port you will soon find yourself at the harbour below. Grey stone houses, hotels, bars, restaurants, cafés and shops lie along the roadway overlooking the sea. Cancale is especially a place for seafood gourmets. For centuries it has been renowned for its shellfish, particularly oysters, the beds of which are cultivated in the shallow bay stretching towards Mont St Michel.

Cancale is also renowned as the birthplace of Jeanne Jugan, founder of the worldwide order of the Little Sisters of the Poor. Jeanne was one of seven and the daughter of a Cancale fisherman. She was left fatherless when still young and worked as a domestic for an elderly lady, who left her 400 francs when she died. Jeanne used this money to buy a home where she could give shelter to poor elderly people. With friends she founded an order which obtained subsistence for their charges entirely by daily begging. This organization, helped by some members of the church, slowly grew. Today there are many thousands of these sisters, working in various establishments, helping to look after the poor.

From St Malo you can make sea excursions to the Channel

Islands, the Ile de Cézembre, the Iles des Chausey (a wild rocky archipelago), and also to Cap Fréhel (a magnificent sea trip) and St Cast.

You can also go by boat down the Rance river to Dinan, a very pleasant trip, as is the bus journey there. The disadvantage of the boat trip (which only takes place during the season) is that it doesn't really give you enough time to see Dinan properly if you intend returning the same day by boat.

Dinan, with its *vieille ville* of half-timbered houses, attractive squares, twisting narrow streets, gardens and trees, is one of the most delightful and best-preserved medieval towns in Brittany. Strategically placed at the head of the Rance estuary, a road-centre of north-east Brittany, it is often referred to as Du Guesclin's town.

This famous Breton military commander, who became constable of France, occupies a rather ambiguous position in Breton history. Although he is esteemed for his success, he cannot really be said to have served the cause of Breton independence, which was pre-served by playing off the English and French kings against each other. Du Guesclin's allegiance to the French king disturbed this delicate balance. He had a hectic career and was taken prisoner several times. On one occasion the French king paid 40,000 crowns for his release, a tidy ransom, proving how useful he found Du Guesclin.

Du Guesclin, who married a Dinan girl, literally left his heart behind him in that town. He had asked to be buried there, so that when he died in 1380 near Châteauneuf de Randon the funeral cortège obediently set off for Dinan. Alas for his wishes, there were many stoppages on the way. His body was embalmed at Le Puy and his entrails left behind in a church there. But as the embalming was badly done the flesh had to be boiled off the bones at Montferrand and buried in a church there. Then a message was received at Le Mans from the king that his skeleton was to be taken and buried in the royal church at St Denis, near Paris. So, in the end, Dinan only received his heart.

It resides in the north arm of St Sauveur's church. If you draw the white curtain before a cenotaph, you will see a carved stone heart, behind which it lies.

Beyond St Sauveur's is its churchyard, now converted into a garden and named rather ironically after Du Guesclin's arch enemies, the English. The Jardin Anglais slopes down among the town's old ramparts towards the river and picturesque old port, not much now used. Above this strides the viaduct bridge, which carries the main road from Paris.

Dinan castle, which has many connections with the Duchess Anne, contains a very good local history museum and is well worth a visit. A lively market is held every Thursday morning in the town.

Elegant Dinard, facing St Malo across the Rance, can also be reached either by boat or road. The road there passes over the top of the famous Rance dam, completed in 1967, the turbines of which use the exceptionally high rise and fall of the tides here to produce electricity. Economically the dam has not proved particularly successful. Nevertheless, as the first sea-powered generating station in the world it is an interesting experiment. There is a car park near by and you can, if you wish, go on a guided tour of the power station.

Dinard, queen of the Emerald Coast, is Brittany's smartest sea resort. It is expensive and staid, yet at the same time gay, with plenty to do (in season, that is; out of season, and this includes June and September, it is rather quiet). It now boasts a new casino with a magnificent dance hall, a large, warmed seawater Olympic swimming pool as well as three splendid beaches, all perfectly safe for bathing. Then its climate is equable, never too hot and never chilly, so that palm trees and exotic flowers grow along its rocky coast.

Unlike St Malo, Dinard is not very old. In fact, if you had come here about a hundred years ago, you would only have seen a small fishing village. Dinard owes its growth to a rich American, a Mr Coppinger, who while out hunting one day with a party from St Malo, unexpectedly came across it. He was so delighted by its good position and wonderfully sandy beaches, that he decided to stay there. Others joined him, and Dinard eventually became a centre for English-speaking people.

It still is, although now many Belgians, Dutch and Germans come, too. There are tea rooms and shops where English is spoken, also an English church and an English library.

One of its chief attractions is that you can walk along its rocky coast without being disturbed by cars. The most famous walk is the Promenade à clair de la lune, which leads down twisting paths to the Pointe du Moulinet (here the Rance meets the sea), from which there is a very good view of Cap Fréhel (on the left) and St Malo (on the right), the Rance Estuary and even Le Grouin in the far distance.

If you continue past here you will come to the Grande Plage, an enormous stretch of sand, overlooked by the new piscine and casino. The main part of the town and the Boulevard Féart lie behind the Grande Plage (also known as the Plage de l'Écluse).

Dinard, like St Malo, is a good centre for excursions. It is also within easy reach of St Lunaire, a smart resort with two beaches, and St Briac, which, along with its picturesque port and pretty pine-fringed beaches, has one of the finest golf courses in Europe. Sailing is popular all along this stretch of coast.

3. Côtes-du-Nord

The Côtes-du-Nord, part of Brittany's northern coastline, with its rocks, cliffs and splendid beaches, is the most popular area of Brittany with British holidaymakers. The people here live chiefly by farming, especially in fertile Tréguier, where you will see fields and fields of yellow ripening corn; and coastal fishing, particularly shellfish, from the countless little ports. The former deepsea and cod fishing were ruined by the fierce competition with Iceland and Norway. Tourism, too, is becoming increasingly important in summer so that numerous villas and hotels now stand beside the small grey stone houses. These are likely to increase now that Britain has joined the Common Market. Perhaps in the future Brittany's ports will connect directly with British ports across the water, as I am sure they must once have done.

However, although the sea, beaches and bathing are such an important feature of this part of Brittany, prospective holiday-makers should bear two things in mind when choosing their place and time.

Firstly, in some places the sea goes out so far that it virtually disappears, leaving behind it a magnificent stretch of golden sand. The swimmer will have to trudge a long way to find it. In fact, there may only be a few hours a day in which to take a swim. So, if you are keen on swimming, find out about tides before choosing your resort.

Secondly, the season is rather short. Out of season includes June and often September. Although the resort will be less crowded, a visit then, even to a large place, will mean that there will be little to do in the evenings. Even the casino may be closed.

The Emerald Coast

As the Emerald Coast lies between the Pointe du Grouin and Val André, it is partly in the Ille et Vilaine department, and partly in Côtes-du-Nord. Although the tourist road does not run beside the sea the whole way, the journey beside this rocky coastline, with its cliffs, wide sandy beaches and high points such as Cap Fréhel, makes a wonderful drive.

Lancieux, first stop of the Côtes-du-Nord when coming from Dinard, is pretty, peaceful, has excellent bathing beaches, and is very suitable for family holidays, as is Jacut-de-la-Mer, situated on a long peninsula projecting into a sheltered bay, safe for boating and with a number of small beaches. It has a picturesque little port. The Guilde, a village surrounded by rocks and cliffs and situated at the mouth of the Arguenon, has a port, too. It also boasts the ruins of a castle, Le Guildo, near by, once the seat of a gallant fifteenth-century poet–noble named Gilles, who was tragically murdered by his brother.

The popular resort of St Cast sprawls out over the peninsula of the same name, which lies between the Arguenon estuary and the bay of Frénaye. It is made up of four parts : Les Mielles, where most of the hotels are to be found; L'Isle, a rocky area, bordering the northern end of its long beach, also with many hotels and villas; Le Bourg, which contains the main public buildings and the old Gothic church; and La Garde, at the beach's southern end, resembling a pretty wooded park. From its point and that of St Cast, there are superb views of the Emerald Coast.

The name St Cast could be Cado or Gattwg (Welsh) and belonged to an Irish priest, born in A.D. 522, who became a bishop. He travelled a great deal, even visiting Palestine and Rome, but finally settled in Brittany, where many places have been named after him. In the Rue de la Colonne you will see a monument surmounted by a greyhound (France) trampling on a leopard

(England). This commemorates the time when British troops who had previously landed in the Bay of St Malo were defeated on St Cast's long beach by French troops under the command of the Duc d'Aiguillon, Governor of Brittany in 1758.

Fort la Latte, which juts out from the next peninsula across the bay of la Frénaye, is best approached from the village of La Motte. Its massive circular keep looks very picturesque and feudal perched on its rocky mound, entered by drawbridges. The castle was built by the Goyon Matignon family in the thirteenth and fourteenth centuries, then restored in the seventeenth. There is a good view of Cap Fréhel from its watch gallery.

Cap Fréhel, over 180 feet high, with its tall red, grey and black cliffs, fringed by wave-battered reefs, is the grand spectacle of the Emerald Coast, and indeed, the finest natural feature of Brittany. It is especially beautiful on a clear evening, when from its top you can glimpse the Channel Islands. You can visit its lighthouse, walk round its cape, and watch the noisy gulls swooping round the curious-shaped Fauconière rocks below.

South-west from Cap Fréhel lies Sables d'Or les Pins, a fairly sophisticated place with a good golf course. It is not a village, more a collection of hotels set amongst pine woods and dunes and with a gorgeous (almost) 3 km. of golden sand beach, all this contributing, of course, to its evocative name. The climate is excellent. But families would probably find Erquy, a near-by pleasant picturesque little fishing port with three beaches, cheaper.

Val André, also a family resort, is very popular with the French, an added recommendation. Its sheltered sandy beach is superb, and one of the best on Brittany's north coast. There is much to do here – tennis, riding, fishing, shooting and especially sailing. There is also horse-racing, a casino and two cinemas and it makes a good centres for walks and excursions.

For history lovers there is the near-by ancient Celtic village of Pléneuf, and a tumulus, dolmen and cromlechs where victims were once sacrificed to the sun. The old fishing port of Dahouët, which lies in a creek beyond the Pointe de la Guette to the west of Val André, was used by the Vikings. Later Breton fishermen practised sailing round here in preparation for their long fishing trips to Newfoundland and Iceland.

The Bay of St Brieuc and the Pink Granite Coast

St Brieuc Bay sweeps down in a rough curve from the Pointe de l'Arcouest, the beginning of the Pink Granite Coast, to Val André.

St Brieuc, situated on the bay of the same name and about 4 km. from the sea, is the business and commercial centre of the Côtes-du-Nord. Busy, prosperous and expanding, with many factories (chiefly for treating and preserving meat and dairy produce), its population has doubled since the end of the war. This once rather charming country town is now surrounded by factories, industrial buildings and estates, so you are not likely to want to spend a holiday there. Nevertheless, because of its airport, railway station, and since it is the point of departure for buses going to seaside resorts or on excursions, you might well find yourself there, perhaps with enough time for a look round.

St Brieuc, founded in the fifth century, is one of the oldest cities in Brittany and is therefore an interesting mixture of old and new. The best place to start your tour of it, is from the Place de la Grille, beside its cathedral, St Étienne (St Stephen). This heavy building is certainly not beautiful, but has a sort of sturdy attraction. The turrets, towers and pepperpot roofs put one in mind of a château-cum-fortress rather than a place of worship. It looks as if it has lived, as indeed it has!

The cathedral occupies the site of an abbey, which was founded at the end of the sixth century by St Brieuc, who came from Cardigan in Wales. Its history has been one of destruction, fire and degradation. It was sacked by the English in 1353, set on fire, used as a fortress, destroyed, rebuilt, damaged again when the Constable de Clisson besieged and captured the town. After being restored and reconstructed during the fifteenth century it was used by the Catholic Leaguers as a refuge for three days in 1592. Its nave nearly collapsed in the eighteenth century. The city's Mayor, Poulain-Carbion, was shot in front of it by the Chouans in 1799.

It was turned into a saltpetre factory during the Revolution, when many of its treasures were burned. It later became a stable for cattle, then a place for storing weapons. As you would expect, such treatment has resulted in a veritable pot-pourri of styles, interesting, but not beautiful. However, it does have a rather fine sixteenth-century organ loft.

If you follow the recommended route through the town, you will next climb the near-by Rue Fardel, passing the old houses, Le Ribault's (fifteenth century) and No. 15, the Hôtel des Ducs de Bretagne (1573), where our James II stayed in 1689. You follow this up to Rue Notre Dame and after continuing along here for a while, turn right into the Rue de la Fontaine St Brieuc. Here a lane leads off to where the old fountain stands, presided over by the Virgin Mary and protected by railings and wire netting. It was once a place of pilgrimage where many sick people came to be cured of their diseases. Behind it is the quaint little chapel of Notre Dame.

If you continue on down the Rue de la Fontaine St Brieuc, and eventually cross over into the Rue Gouet, you will soon find yourself back in the Place de la Grille, opposite the cathedral.

If you still have time to spare, you can visit the Boulevard Lamartine; from the roundabout at its end you will have a good view of the valley. A better view still can be had from the Tertre Aubé at the opposite end of the Boulevard Lamartine, continuing along the Boulevards Gambetta and Pasteur. From here you can see the valleys, the Bay of St Brieuc and the Tour de Cesson in the far distance. This is the remains of a fourteenth-century fort which was built on the site of a Roman camp. It was captured by de Mercoeur's Catholic forces after much difficulty during the Wars of Religion, but after 1598 was returned to Henri IV. On the request of the people of St Brieuc the French king had it blown up.

St Brieuc is situated on a plateau divided by two waterways, the Gouëdic and the Gouet. A good view of the Gouëdic valley with its viaducts can be seen from the Rond Point Huguin, not far from Tertre Aubé. From here you can also see the coast as far as Cap

Fréhel. A granite monument to Anatole Le Braz, Brittany's great folklorist, stands in the little park. He is shown in a familiar pose, listening to his companion, Margaret Philippe, who is telling him an old Breton legend. From here, you can return to the town by Rue Victor Hugo, Boulevard Thiers and the Grandes Promenades, an attractive public garden which encircles the Courts of Justice. There is an open air theatre and children's playground here.

St Brieuc is useful for shopping. Campers should note that there is a fish market every day in the Place du Martray, also a market for fruit and vegetables.

Northwards from St Brieuc the road is somewhat uninteresting. The coast is not much indented and there are only a few ports and family resorts.

Binic is a small, quite attractive fishing port. Étaples is a family resort with two good sandy beaches. St Quay-Portrieux, a fishing port and resort which have joined together, is larger, popular with people of fairly modest means (especially those with small children), has good sandy beaches, a casino, miniature golf course, cinemas and facilities for tennis, fishing and sailing. Plouha, situated about 3 km. from the sea, where there are good safe beaches, is quieter and also suitable for family holidays. Brittany is France's chief reservoir for sailors and many naval pensioners live around this area, who supplement their income by cultivating plots of land and letting off parts of their houses in summer.

Paimpol, which gained fame through Pierre Loti's novel *Pêcheur d'Islande*, is a picturesque port with quaint old streets and houses. In its heyday it was the base for a great cod fleet, whose ships ventured as far as Newfoundland and Iceland. Today, although coastal fishing still continues, as does oyster cultivation, its harbour is mostly filled with yachts. The town is also a centre for early vegetables. Still, there is a bit to remind you of its former grandeur, such as a museum of the sea and oyster cultivation, and a merchant seamen's college. Paimpol attracts many artists and writers and will appeal to those who like rugged holidays with plenty of fishing, sailing and boat trips.

From here you can visit the rocky seascape, the Pointe de

l'Arcouest, then take the ferry boat across to the island of Bréhat. You can also take a boat direct to Bréhat from Paimpol.

Bréhat, which is about 3½ km. long and 1½ km. wide, is really made up of two islands joined by a narrow strip of land. Surrounded by islets and reefs its rugged pink granite coast makes a strong contrast with the blue-green sea.

It is a little Eden, where mimosa, fig and palm trees flourish, its peacefulness undisturbed by mundane cars, for they are not allowed on the island. It seldom rains as the rain clouds usually miss it out on their way to the mainland.

You will arrive at Port Clos, about a kilometre from Le Bourg, the 'town'. You can tour the island through the rocks by boat, or you can just wander over it, perhaps visiting the lighthouse, the Phare de Paon. But everywhere is interesting.

Bréhat was once a busy port for sea traffic. Tradition has it that a sea captain from here, while staying in Lisbon, met Christopher Columbus and told him how the island fishermen made their way to the New World, via Newfoundland.

The drive from Paimpol, crossing two bridges, to Tréguier, an old town and port overlooking the junction of the Jaudy and Guindy rivers, is a pleasant one. This area is part of the Trégorois, which is renowned for the production of early vegetables.

Tréguier, once the capital of Trégor and an episcopal city, is an interesting old town with plenty of quiet character. Its cathedral (although now termed a church) of St Tugdual, is one of the best known in the province. This fine Gothic building with its three towers (one Romanesque) and beautiful cloisters (a frequent subject of paintings), dominates the town from the centre of its square.

Its patron saint is St Yves, one of Brittany's most popular saints, for he was traditionally the righter of wrongs and advocate of the poor.

Yves Hélori, born in 1253 at Minihy Tréguier not far from the town, was the son of a country gentleman. He was always interested in religion and after studying law in Paris, where he stayed for 13 years, returned to Brittany to become a priest. He also became a magistrate and advocate in the Bishop of Tréguier's ecclesiastical court, which tried civil cases as well. He soon became famous as the poor man's lawyer, choosing only to help the most wretched cases. He was canonized only 45 years after his death. Since then he has always been known as the patron saint of lawyers. You will see many statues of him in Breton churches. The favourite one shows him standing between a poor man and a rich man, whose purse he is refusing.

A church has been built over the manor in which he was born and died, and which is now the scene of a famous annual Pardon. Pilgrims are expected to scramble through a low thirteenth-century archway, known as St Yves's 'tomb' in the centre of the cemetery on their knees.

Tréguier was also the birthplace of another Breton celebrity, but one of a rather different type. Ernest Renan, philosopher and historian, made science his religion. His book *The Life of Christ* and others were roundly condemned by the Roman Catholic church. Even so, his statue has the place of honour in the square in front of the 'cathedral'. His humble home and birthplace have been turned into a museum.

Perros Guirec, on the coast, not easy to reach by bus from Tréguier, is one of Brittany's largest resorts. From here begins the Corniche Bretonne (Breton coast road), one of the most interesting parts of the Pink Granite Coast. Around here granite rocks have been chipped and chiselled by that great artist the sea, helped by the wind and the rain. Locals have given these strange shapes names, some eerie, such as The Witch and Death's Head; some are creatures, such as The Rabbit and The Tortoise; others are more mundane, such as The Thimble, The Umbrella, The Cork-screw, The Armchair, and there is even a Napoleon's Hat.

Perros Guirec, like Quay-Portrieux, was formed by two joined-up villages. The name Perros comes from the old word Pen Roz, while Guirec was called after an early priest, St Guirec. Today, it is an expensive and fashionable resort, boasting a casino and two good beaches, but rather dull out of season.

I liked its odd-looking, squat, sturdy little church partly

Romanesque (twelfth century) and partly Gothic (fourteenth century), built out of granite and topped by a tower and spire. Also, the pinkish chapel, Notre-Dame-de-la-Clarté (sixteenth century) on a hill is worth seeing. Apparently a Breton noble, whose ship was lost in a fog off this coast, vowed that he would build a chapel on whatever part of the coast showed first to give him his bearings. To commemorate this, the chapel was named Our Lady of Light.

The Plage Trestraou, an enormous sweep of sand, with a casino behind, reminded me of Dinard, except that the very solid granite seats on the promenade were proof positive that one was now well and truly into Brittany. Perhaps, too, the sand is a little paler.

However, the best part of Perros Guirec, the real *pièce de résistance*, in my view, anyway, is the fascinating walk along the Sentier des Douaniers (the Coastguards' Patrol).

Its start lies behind the Rue de la Clarté, or you can take the steps up beside the left of the Ecole de la Voile, on the Plage Trestraou. This walk, which takes about one and a quarter hours, follows the cliff, first along winding grassy paths, then slopes down to the rocky shore and varied-shaped, pink and grey rocks. They are all fantastical, out-surrealizing any creations by Barbara Hepworth and Henry Moore. Some must surely be crouching, petrified monsters, left stranded by the sea, others, piles of pink stones, are perhaps the start of some piscine palace, left carelessly to be used later. You pass many little caves and pools, secret and private, while in the distance looms the lighthouse. A park, a sort of rock reserve, lies behind granite posts. On the far side, near the beach of St Guirec, stands the small oratory dedicated to this saint, who is supposed to have landed here in the sixth century.

When I visited this place one evening, it was at its eerie best, an enchanted and ageless spot, surrounded by an atmosphere of primitive, prehistoric magic. One expected the wizard Merlin in his tall cap suddenly to emerge from the shadows and dance round with the ghoulies and korrigans. Perhaps the few crosses that have been planted on the rocks have been put there to offset their mischief and protect the unwary visitor from their attentions.

My path eventually led me to a secluded silent beach, which led into a small port and the little town of Ploumanach. From here, I was able to catch a bus back to Perros Guirec.

Trégastel Plage, the next resort to Ploumanach, also has its share of strange-shaped rocks. To the right of its Coz Pors beach are a pile known as the Tortues ('tortoises'). Above them stands a statue of the eternal father, and below, caves with a prehistoric museum in one. From the Grève Blanche (white shore), which you can reach by taking the rocky path round the promontory, you can see Rabbits Island and the Triagoz islands, also the rock called The Corkscrew, and the great shape supposed to resemble a crown, which is known as the Roi Gradlon crown.

At Trégastel Bourg, a few kilometres from the Plage, is an interesting twelfth–thirteenth-century church and its seventeenth-century ossuary. Just outside the village is a calvary, standing on a little hill. From here there is a very good view of the coast.

There are many islands off this part of the coast, the largest being Ile Grand, which is connected to the mainland by a road. The most distant, the Sept Iles about five miles out at sea, have a lighthouse and a bird sanctuary.

Trébeurden, lying farther south along the coast, is another larger seaside resort, also rocky and with good beaches. The Tresmeur beach is the most popular.

Lannion, which lies inland on the Léguer river, is the commercial centre of this area, linking as it does both with Tréguier and Guincamp, and is a good place from which to start on excursions farther afield. There is not much to see in the town itself – medieval houses in the Place du Général-Leclerc and the Brélévenez church, which was built on a hill by the Templars in the twelfth century. Near by, are the châteaux of Kergrist (you can only visit outside) and Tonquédec (an impressive ruin) and the Chapelle de Kerfons (fifteenth-century, prettily situated). Or for those who are more interested in the present and future, there is the space and telecommunications centre at Pleumeur-Bodou, whose white plastic sphere can be seen from afar.

For trips into Brittany's interior, the town of Guincamp makes a good centre. From here you can get to Mur-de-Bretagne, just in

Côtes-du-Nord, which makes a good starting place for a tour of Lake Guerlédan (see chapter 5).

The Corniche de l'Amorique (Amorican coast road) starts from St Michel-en-Grève, a small seaside resort, renowned for its sailors' church and cemetery, prettily situated beside the sea. Next to it stretches a magnificent three-mile beach, the Lieue de Grève ('league of shore'). The road here is very picturesque as it follows the wooded coast, passing the Grand Rocher, then St Efflam, which joins up with Plestin-les-Grèves, farther inland. The road between St Efflam and Locquirec, following the ragged coast, is particularly attractive. When you arrive at the little fishing port and resort of Locquirec Côtes-du-Nord has ended. You are now in Finistère, the mysterious land of the west.

8   Quimper cathedral from the southwest

4. Finistère

Finistère, the old west Brittany of legends, of winds and wide skies, or rough seas and rocks, of rivers, forests, and 'mountains' is for those who like rugged yet relaxing holidays.

It does not have one central town you can pinpoint as capital, but three, Morlaix, capital of the north, Brest, capital of the north-west, and Quimper (pronounced Kempair), capital of the south.

Morlaix and its surroundings

Morlaix, an attractive old town, climbing steep valley walls, lies at the foot of a high viaduct bridge crossed by a railway. The town grew up round the Rivière de Morlaix, beyond the viaduct, and was once quite a prosperous and important port. Today, its harbour is used chiefly for pleasure yachts, or boats carrying market produce, such as fruit and vegetables, especially strawberries.

Sleepy Morlaix existed during Roman times. During the twelfth century it was one of the residences of the counts of Brittany. An incident which took place in the early sixteenth century enabled its inhabitants to add a lion facing a leopard (English) and the probably practical if rather unchristian motto *'S'ils te mordent, mord les'* ('If they bite you, bite them') to their coat of arms.

The English fleet, which sailed up the estuary in 1522 to anchor below the town, had been told that the nobles and merchants, its chief defenders, were away attending the great fair of Noyal, near Pontivy. No doubt they thought they had a good chance of getting some easy booty.

According to local legend, they enjoyed themselves too much and stayed too long and were therefore caught red-handed by the returning people. They were too befuddled to defend themselves, so victory was easy. A further attack, this time in 1532 by corsairs, decided the Morlaisiens to construct the Château du Taureau ('Bull's Castle') strategically at the entrance to the estuary in 1544.

Because of its many old twisting, steep, narrow streets, Morlaix can really only be explored properly on foot. It is a pleasant place just to wander round in. I suggest you first visit the Syndicat d'Initiative, placed very conveniently at the foot of the viaduct in the Place des Otages, where you will get a map and much helpful information. Nearby is quite a cheap restaurant and bar, the Café Moderne.

If you climb to the right of the viaduct, passing an old seventeenth-century house with dormer windows, you will find yourself outside St Melaine, a fifteenth-century, Gothic Flamboyant church. Its square steeple, shouldered by buttresses, is topped by a modern spire. Inside, the chief treasures are its modern stained glass windows and a colourful tableau representing the descent from the cross.

St Melaine was originally an old priory, founded in the twelfth century, as was St Mathieu, on the opposite side of the old part of the town, which was demolished in 1821 and rebuilt (except for a sixteenth-century tower) in 1824. St Mathieu possesses rather an unusual treasure, a fifteenth-century statue of the Virgin, which opens to reveal a figure holding Christ on the cross inside (over the altar to the left of the high altar). The thirteenth-century church of the Jacobins in the Place des Jacobins was badly damaged during the Revolution, when it was used as a stable and storage loft; it now contains a museum.

In spite of numerous depredations over the centuries, Morlaix still has some attractive sixteenth-century gabled houses. The gracious house of Duchess Anne, 33 Rue du Mur, with three overhanging timbered stories, is the best. Its closed court inside has a lantern roof. There is also a very fine carved staircase and a remarkable chimney along one wall. Other picturesque old houses and low-fronted shops with broad windows are situated in the narrow street, rather ironically named the Grande Rue.

Morlaix is especially the happy hunting ground for history-loving holidaymakers. All around and within easy reach are some of Brittany's finest churches, chapels and most elaborate calvaries. One of the most popular excursions you can take from this centre is the one to the *enclos paroissiaux*, the parish closes.

During the season there are special excursions; otherwise you can drive round them by car, or take a local bus. The chief parishes to visit are St Thégonnec, Guimiliau, and Lampaul.

When staying at Morlaix, I took a local bus to St Thégonnec, the best of the three parish enclosures, standing magnificently in the centre of its village. As it was out of season the priest who usually showed people round was absent, but he had thoughtfully left all the relevant information on the chapel steps.

It told me, of course, what I already knew, that these buildings were an open air museum and formed the most complete and splendid enclosure in all Brittany. They had taken two centuries to build (1550–1750) and were a masterpiece in praise of God, built by local people who had not hesitated to devote a large part of their wealth, acquired by flax growing and weaving, to its construction.

'Now stand in the middle of the road, but mind the traffic,' the notice said, which I obeyed, although fortunately there wasn't much around just then.

The rounded triumphal arch before me symbolized the victorious entry of a Christian, redeemed by Christ into the immortality of a heavenly Jerusalem. A statue of the Heavenly Father stood in its centre to welcome me inside.

Once through its arch, I examined the calvary, built in 1610, which tells the story in carved figures of Christ's trial, crucifixion and redemption, and it was quite fascinating. It was easy to see how a priest could use it as a teaching aid – also as political propaganda. Henri IV, because he was a Protestant and anti-Leaguer (Catholics), is shown as an executioner. The face of Christ and the faces of his friends always looked divine and at peace, while those of his enemies wore foolish and malicious grins. Above the carved tableaux of figures rose three crosses and two horsemen who kept watch over the crucified figure at its summit. Below the crosses four angels collected blood in chalices.

The church was fascinating, too, and its tower (begun 1599 and still incomplete in 1626) is one of the best examples of a Breton Renaissance tower. The most beautiful thing inside it is the exquisitely carved pulpit 'fit for a pope and not an inch of oak wasted', which was done by two brothers, François and Guillaume Lerrel in 1683. Above it is a canopy, covered in carved cherubs and roses, on top of which fame blows a trumpet.

The statue of St Thégonnec stands in a niche over the pulpit, while on the left-hand side of the church is the colourful St Pol-de-Léon (patron saint of Léon), with the defeated dragon of paganism lying at his feet.

St Pol-de-Léon also stands above the entrance door to the ossuary outside the church. Ossuaries were originally bone houses: bodies were removed from their coffins after a number of years of burial, and their skulls arranged along the shelves, the name of each owner being written across it in black paint. Later the ossuaries were turned into chapels of rest where bodies were kept before burial.

St Thégonnec's ossuary, built in 1676, is now an ornate and magnificent chapel. Below Joseph and the boy Jesus, surmounted by the eternal father, steps descend to an extremely vivid tableau of life-size figures. It shows the Descent from the Cross, the most popular of Breton religious scenes. The crucified Christ is surrounded by mourning figures, among them Mary Magdalene, particularly overwhelmed by sorrow.

Guimiliau is the next place to visit after St Thégonnec, that is if you are doing the tour properly, or have a car. But if you are relying on local transport, you will be unlucky. It seems that the rivalry between St Thégonnec and Guimiliau is so great that you must make your choice, and visit either one or the other. There is no public transport link between them although a train runs through St Guimiliau (no ticket office, though, you must pay on the train or at the other end). St Thégonnec's station is about five kilometres from the village. The walk from St Thégonnec to Guimiliau is about 10 km.

Guimiliau's calvary, with its 200 figures (built 1581 to 1588) is the largest and certainly the most famous in Brittany. On its uppermost part is a large cross; the four statues on its shafts are the Virgin and St John, and St Peter and St Yves. There are scenes from the passion on its platform and a tableau showing the story of Catell Gollett (Kathleen the Lost). As this story was quite often told as a warning to naughty flirtatious girls by priests, I will relate it.

Kathleen was a young servant girl, who didn't TELL ALL at confession. From this small beginning and lapse, she started on the slippery slope and became really wicked, one day actually stealing some consecrated bread to give to her lover. Unfortunately for her, he was really the devil in disguise. For this dreadful deed she was condemned to eternal hellfire.

The sixteenth-century church, rebuilt in flamboyant Renaissance style at the beginning of the seventeenth century, is worth seeing, especially its south porch and the fine carved oak baptistry, pulpit and organ loft. The ossuary chapel is quite interesting, but not up to the standard of St Thégonnec.

Lampaul, not far from Guimiliau, also has a parish close worth seeing. The interior of this church is particularly harmonious and contains some treasures, such as a very fine baptismal font, a decorated sixteenth-century rood beam crossing the nave, and a representation of the entombment.

For those who prefer rocks and wooded walks, Huelgoat, in the Monts d'Arrée, about 29 km. from Morlaix, can also be visited by local bus. Picturesquely situated beside a lake and forest, the remains of the old Argoat, it is renowned for its odd-shaped rocks, grottoes, underground river and waterfalls.

Huelgoat, with its large square with an old fountain in the centre, does not itself have very much to offer the tourist. There is the Renaissance chapel of Notre Dame des Cieux, rather dilapidated outside and bare within, which has some bas reliefs of

life of the Virgin and Passion which are of interest, as are the
curious faces sticking out of the wooden beam running round the
top of the walls. The church in the square is very plain, although
it does contain a rather good example of St Yves, patron saint of
Huelgoat, receiving a poor man's petition while refusing a rich
man's purse. This church also has a very loud ticking clock, which
must make services difficult to hear.

So when you arrive by car or bus the first thing to make for is
the rocks. Follow the Rue des Cendres down as far as the white
Café du Chaos, opposite a garage, and not far from the large
lake. I am putting in these instructions because the path, in spite
of a plaque beside the café, is narrow and easily missed.

You follow it and suddenly find yourself in another world, a
world of enormous mossy green boulders humped around the
noisy underground river, a place well-named the Chaos du
Moulin.

It is slippery and slimy and you have to squeeze past boulders
and scramble up and down rough stairs. But the places to see are
well-marked – La Grotte du Diable, to which you descend some
steps, then a ladder, to gaze into the grotto and underground
stream below. There is also a Théâtre du Verdu, set among trees
and surrounded by rocks. Beyond this are steps and paths leading
from a wide path over the hill, all finding the way eventually to
the Roche Tremblante ('trembling rock'), a large 100-ton boulder,
which is supposed to sway when touched but I'm afraid I did not
have the knack. If you return to the wide path and continue along
it you come to the next natural sight – the Ménage de la Vierge
('Virgin's kitchen'). There are certainly some strange indentures in
the rocks round about, but you will have to use your imagination
about this.

The wide path also leads to the Sentier des Amoureux 'lovers'
path') on the left. It is easy to see how this got its name, as the
path seems to wander vaguely in many different directions, which
mostly end nowhere in particular, such as tiny glens, and one soon
loses one's way. However, if you bear right at the first fork and
keep on what looks like the main path, you will eventually find

first. La Grotte d'Artus, a large grotto, made from a tumble of boulders, then the Mare aux Sangliers ('Boars' pool'), a pretty pool fed by two small waterfalls, crossed by a bridge. The Allée Violette, which is approached from the main path, is a very pleasant forest walk, beside the underground river, which, after roaring below the boulders, gradually widens out into a visible stream. The path ends on the road, which you can take back to Huelgoat.

Or you can continue on down it, through the forest. If you intend to do any further walks, it would be as well to get a map and booklet from the Syndicat d'Initiative in the main square. The walk alongside the canal is a very popular one.

Apart from its strange-shaped rocks, and forest walks, Huelgoat makes a good starting place for a tour of the Monts d'Arrée, Brittany's highest 'mountains'. This range, once much higher, has gradually been eroded down the centuries, some parts turning into rounded hills (*ménez*), others becoming sharp, fretted crests (roc'hs). They are often hidden behind mists and appear rather bare and bleak, although those to the east are more wooded. From the heights there are some good views of the surrounding countryside.

The heights of the Monts d'Arrée can be toured by car (about 120 km.), starting from Huelgoat, passing Roc Trévezel, very picturesque against its mountain background, then to Montagne St Michel and the oak and beech forests of Granou. From Le Faou, a picturesquely situated town at the head of the Faou estuary, which looks best at high tide, you can return to Huelgoat via Pleyben, renowned for its splendid parish close and calvary. Brasparts also has an interesting parish close, as does St Herbot. St Herbot's church is of interest because he was the patron saint of horned cattle, and before St Herbot's Pardon, in May, farmers place tufts of hair taken from their cattle's tails on two stone tables beside its carved oak screen.

Huelgoat is about 21 km. from Carhaix, which was an important town in Roman times (the old capital of Finistère). It is still a junction of roads and now of railways, too, and as it lies in the centre of a cattle-breeding area it is renowned for its cattle fairs. Carhaix also makes a good centre to start on a tour of the Montagnes Noires.

Lying to the south-east, this range has somewhat lower and less steep slopes than the Monts d'Arrée. Dark firs cover many of its sides, which is why it is called black. Here you are in the real heart of Brittany and are likely to hear Breton spoken. If you wish to tour this area, Châteauneuf du Faou, a pretty village, is a good place to stay at and use as an excursion centre. Both the Montagnes Noires and the Monts d'Arrée are excellent areas for fishing.

Morlaix to Roscoff; St Pol-de-Léon

Roscoff, which can be reached quite easily by bus or train from Morlaix, also makes a pleasant car drive. At first, that is when the road follows the river, passing Carentec, a delightful seaside resort, situated on a cape between the estuary of the Penzé and Morlaix.

Later though it becomes rather dull. You will pass through St Pol-de-Léon, now an important market town for artichokes, cauliflowers, onions and potatoes, but whose cathedral and Kreisker tower bring a touch of grandeur to the surrounding flat countryside.

The name St Pol comes from Paulus Aurelianus, a Cambrian monk who landed here in the sixth century from Wales. He founded a monastery, became an abbot, then bishop. St Pol-de-Léon had the honour of being the first bishopric in Lower Brittany.

The present cathedral, built in the thirteenth century, replacing an earlier Romanesque one, has great elegance, especially in the façade with its huge porch and three high windows above. The whole building has a great purity of style. The interior also shows harmonious design – a nave of seven bays with a network of 12 slender columns and sixteenth-century Gothic stalls.

St Paul's bones are preserved in a chalice opposite the great rose window. There are tombs of many bishops, including that of Jean

François de la Marche, an émigré along with Chateaubriand in London who helped to administer a fund for the assistance of dependants of those killed in the Quiberon expedition. He died in 1806, when his remains were taken to his see in St Pol-de-Léon. English people might be interested to know that he wrote 'The generosity of the English nation surpasses all the instances of benevolences recorded in the history of nations'. Alas, the bishopric of St Pol-de-Léon did not survive Napoleon. The old palace of the bishops is now the Town Hall.

The chapel of the Kreisker, near by, dates from the fourteenth century, but was altered and enlarged in the following century and was used as a chapel by the Town Council. Now it is the college chapel, but it is its beautiful belfry, so delicate and slender, a marvel of balance which has served as a model for many other Breton towers, which has made the Kreisker chapel famous. It may be climbed – 169 steps if you feel energetic – and you will be rewarded by a very fine panoramic view of the surrounding countryside.

Roscoff

Roscoff, with its mild climate and streets of sturdy grey stone houses, is one of my favourite little seaside towns in Brittany. It is likely to become many other people's favourite, too, now that the shipping line between it and Plymouth for travellers and cars together is in action. Holidaymakers coming to Brittany will find it a convenient place to land in if they intend staying in Finistère or the western end of the Côtes-du-Nord.

The port looks out across seaweed-covered rocks to the island of Batz. To get there is very simple. You just walk down a long narrow way, which eventually drops down, covered in green slime, into the sea. Near its end is a little white boat with a blue cabin, the *Santa Anna*, which makes a 15-minute journey to the island about once every hour.

From a distance, Batz looks quite an important place. Its tall lighthouse put me in mind of Nelson's column. But on closer acquaintance it is a mere fishing village, with tiny grey stone houses divided by narrow cobbled streets, bleak yet attractive. Most of the men are sailors, while the women work in the fields or collect seaweed. This, when processed with shells and sea mud, is used as a fertilizer, and its collection is quite an important industry all along this part of the coast.

Batz, sheltered by reefs on its north side, is treeless, but to prove that it is on the Gulf Stream it has a garden of tropical plants on its south-west point. It has some sandy beaches, unlike Roscoff's, which are shingle. If you like rugged picturesqueness and extreme quiet, you might enjoy a holiday on Batz.

Most people connect Roscoff with onion sellers, and certainly it is a great centre for vegetables, especially cauliflowers and artichokes, grown all around in the area known as the Ceinture Dorée ('golden belt'); fish, too – apart from being an important lobster port, Roscoff's Charles Pérez Aquarium, which shows sea creatures in their natural environment, is the most important marine laboratory in France.

Roscoff has another claim to fame in that it possesses an enormous, nearly 360-year-old fig tree, which can produce as much as 1,000 lbs of figs a year; it grows in a Capuchin convent garden.

Like St Malo, Roscoff was once a centre for corsairs. Sculpted ships and cannons decorate the outside walls and towers of its sixteenth-century church, Notre Dame de Kroaz-Baz, around which the old town clusters. It also has a remarkable Renaissance belfry with three towers representing the Trinity, reckoned to be one of the finest in Finistère.

Roscoff should be of interest to the Scots for it was here that the five-year-old child, Mary Stuart, landed in 1548 on her way to her betrothed, the young French dauphin. A turret marks the place where she landed – the old harbour has been considerably changed since then. But you can still see the plain grey stone house where she is supposed to have spent her first night in France. Nearly 200 years later, another Scot, Charles Edward Stuart, the Young Pretender, also landed here after his disastrous defeat at Culloden, pursued to the last by English ships.

My last impression was of Scotland again, because there were bagpipes playing what sounded like a Highland Fling as I sat on a bus waiting to go to Brest. The driver reminded me that bagpipes were Breton, too, and that the International Bagpipe Festival, held for three days in Brest every August, is one of the biggest folklore festivals in Brittany.

So we started our journey, most appropriately to the skirl of pipes and with seagulls whirling overhead in a grey sky. The driver was an amusing fellow, very cheerful and friendly, shaking hands with all who got on the bus, and waving to those who didn't. Even the dogs weren't left out – he barked at them. Nor for that matter were the cows; every time we passed a field of them he made a noise on his mouthpiece which sounded just like a moo. They all stared at the bus with uncomprehending astonishment. Our drive to Brest first through flat fields of vegetables, later through a more varied undulating countryside, was certainly a spirited one. He almost danced the bus down the road. Fortunately, there was little traffic about at that time.

Brest and its surroundings

I am afraid I have a rather jaundiced opinion of Brest. This is partly due to the fact that it was pouring with rain when I arrived and partly because I had difficulty in finding a hotel; the Syndicat d'Initiative, when I found it, was closed, and the people who should have been there were all away attending a fair somewhere else. I also met a dripping wet young American couple at the station who told me they hated the place. 'It's really dull. We're just getting the hell out of it.'

But I think their judgment was a bit harsh. Brest suffered very badly during the last war and has been completely rebuilt. It is now a modern, well-laid-out city with good shops, parks and wide boulevards. But although all this probably makes it more comfortable to live in it is rather featureless, and not for the tourist in search of local colour.

It owes much to Colbert (1619–83), one of France's great

ministers, who made it the maritime capital of France. The marine and administration office, now known as the Inscription Maritime Office, set up by him, still exists today. He also founded a school of gunnery, a college of marine guards, a school of hydrography and a school for marine engineers. Out of all this emerged France's powerful fleet. Other things were added later, such as better dockyards, buoy moorings, and Vauban's strong fortifications.

Brest, although now an important commercial centre with a well-known university, is still predominantly a city of the sea. Its position is uniquely good : the harbour, the total anchorage of which covers about 50 square miles and is 40 feet deep in parts, connects with many inlets and also with the Atlantic through the Goulet channel.

Unfortunately, Brest's first-class strategic position was also her undoing. During the Second World War she was invaluable to the Germans as a submarine base, and a great worry to the Allied convoys sailing between Britain and America. The result was a long and intensive bombardment. All this, added to the Germans' destroying much of the centre before the Americans moved in, resulted in a devastated, almost gutted city.

The Bretons are proud of the new one that has arisen from the ashes. In fact, it was often quoted to me as being the most beautiful city in their province. Whether it is or not, I do not feel competent to judge – most of the time I stayed there it was shrouded in mist.

On my second day there, when it had lifted just enough to allow one to see where one was going, I walked to the Cours Dajot, a small park on the hill, from which there is a grand view over the roadstead and harbour. That you can see see the mouth of the Élorn river, the Ménez Hom and the Pointe du Portzic I take on trust : the viewing table said you could.

There are some quite good excursions by bus, car or boat from Brest. You can drive, or take a bus, to the Pointe St Mathieu, whose tall lighthouse stands amid the ruins of a sixth-century Benedictine abbey, and then visit Le Conquet, a rugged picturesque little fishing port and resort, the southern extremity of the grim northern promontory of Finistère. Or, going in the opposite direction, you can drive over Pont Albert Louppe to the Plougastel peninsula, a little old-world area of Brittany, famous for its strawberries. Plougastel-Daolas, the chief town, possesses quite a famous calvary, built at the beginning of the seventeenth century as a thanksgiving for the ending of the plague. The modern church beside it has a brilliantly coloured interior.

Then there are the Abers. *Aber* is the Breton word (Welsh, too) for estuary. This north-west promontory of Finistère, bleak and wild, is broken by rivers and innumerable shallow streams, which wind across its low-lying hills. Its rocky coastline is dotted with tiny islands, rich in seaweed. This coast of legends, often hidden behind mists, has a sort of melancholy charm, and makes quite an attractive tour.

L'Aber Wrach on the west side is a smartish yachting centre. Le Folgoët, lying inland on its eastern side, is particularly renowned for its large, square-shaped church and beautiful belfry (a copy of the Kreisker one at St Pol-de-Léon). Its Pardon, which takes place in September, attracts some of the largest numbers in Brittany. Find time to visit the church. Note the delicate rood screen, also the fountain in the chapel porch, presided over by the Virgin Mary. Its waters come from a spring under the altar.

And herein lies a story. According to tradition, a simple fellow, named Salaün (Solomon), usually known as Folgoët ('fool of the wood'), lived near a spring in the wood. He only knew a few words, which were 'O, Lady Virgin Mary' (in Breton, of course), which he was always repeating. He died eventually but the people were surprised to find a white lily growing in the woods with these words showing in the design of its pistils. Curious, they dug up the lily and were utterly amazed to discover that the flower was growing out of the fool's mouth. The War of Succession was taking place then, and the Duke of Montfort had made a vow that if he won, he would build a great church to the Virgin. After his victory at Auray, it was decided that this would be the place to put it. The altar was set over the spring from which the idiot drank.

South of the church lies the sixteenth-century manor house, called the Doyenné, now containing a museum. This was where the Duchess Anne stayed when she came on a pilgrimage here in the early sixteenth century. There is also an inn near by where pilgrims stayed.

Not far from Le Folgoët stands the château of Kerjean, partly a fortress, guarded by a moat and thick walls, and partly a Renaissance palace with decorated rooms, colonnades, park and fountain. Kerjean, which was bought by the state in 1911, now contains a small museum of Breton furniture. The *lits clos* (box beds) are like tiny rooms in themselves. There are also some amusing stories connected with the old residents of this house.

If you wish to make a sea trip from Brest (weather permitting), the Port du Commerce lies on the left-hand side of the station and about 1 km. down the hill. You will pass the red granite obelisk in the Cours Dajot, erected by the United States to commemorate the achievements of the French and United States naval forces during the war. The original monument was to World War One, but was destroyed by the Germans in 1941. This one was erected in 1958.

There is not much to see in the port for the most interesting part of the harbour – the naval dockyards, arsenal and castle – are not for prying foreign eyes. However, if you walk as far as the wall on the right you will see gaunt grey battleships lying in dock, below the old château on the other side of the town and bay, while loudspeakers shout instructions to sailors engaged on various mysterious naval activities.

Tickets for the Vedettes Amoricaines are obtained from a new blue-and-white office beside a small port. You can go to Le Conquet by boat as well as bus, and the Ile d'Ouessant (Ushant) if you have the time (it takes about four hours to get there) and a strong stomach, for the sea can be very rough.

Ouessant, the rocky island on the extreme north-west corner of Brittany is notorious for the perilous currents and reefs surrounding it. It is particularly dangerous to approach in winter because of fog and high winds, and has been the scene of many shipwrecks.

Even so, its climate is very mild. If you managed to get there in January and February you would find yourself in one of the warmest parts of France. It is familiar to British sailors because its powerful Créac'h lighthouse, along with the one on Bishop Rock, marks the beginning of the English Channel.

On the way there the boat stops at Le Conquet and the tiny island of Molène, lying amid an archipelago of rocks and islets. Ouessant is about 16 square km. and Lampaul is its largest settlement. Here, you should have a meal of shellfish and salt mutton, the island's two culinary specialities. Most of the land is given over to grazing sheep. As with Batz, the women cultivate what crops there are, while the men are sailors or fishermen (mostly of lobsters).

The Crozon peninsula can be reached either by road (quite a long journey) or by boat (three-quarters of an hour), but you can only buy your ticket half an hour before the voyage in case of bad weather. I left Brest this second way and caught the small white steamer to Le Fret opposite. From here I was told there would be a coach connection with Crozon and Morgat beyond.

It was a pleasant crossing giving one a good general view of the roadstead, also Brest, with its old castle, busy docks, and tall modern buildings. Eventually, one could see the coast in outline as far as Pte. St Mathieu and Pont Albert Louppe, which links the mainland with the Plougastel peninsula.

The Crozon Peninsula

The coach at Le Fret turned out to be a small van into which everyone was squeezed, along with a pig (fortunately, dead). The countryside through which we drove was rather wild and wooded with frequent stretches of ferns and gorse and appeared deserted.

The Crozon peninsula, which stretches out like a tongue between Brittany's western extremities, the Abers and Cornouaille, has one of the best and warmest climates in Brittany. Moreover, it is still largely undiscovered by British holidaymakers.

Morgat, once a sardine port, is its most popular resort, because of its large, safe, sandy beach, set in a sheltered bay. I found it attractive and homely, a good centre for walks along the cliffs, sailing (there is a yacht club and school), fishing and seafood restaurants. Then there are its grottoes. The small caves which lie at the foot of a spur between Morgat and Le Portzic beaches can be reached at low tide, while the large ones have to be visited by motor boat (you can get one from the port and it takes about three-quarters of an hour). There are two groups of these. The best grotto is the beautifully coloured one called the Altar (250 feet deep and 45 feet high).

The chief drawback about Morgat, though, is its bus service (only one a day when I was there), so if you want to make excursions farther afield and you have no car, you will have to walk three kilometres to Crozon, the administrative and geographical centre of the small peninsula.

There was once a Crozon–Morgat railway station. This is now, alas, a mere façade standing in front of a derelict track, a reminder that it was one of Brittany's uneconomic lines. The plain grey ex-railway station now houses an SNCF bus office: the yard in front is the starting place of Crozon's few buses.

Crozon, old, grey and typically Breton, was known in the fifth century as Crauthon, which later became Crauzon. It is built round its long plain church, the rounded tower of which peers like a prim governess above the houses, a landmark for miles.

Unlike so many churches in other places, Breton ones are often in use, even on a weekday morning. There are no plaques or statues inside to important people, apart from Bishops, who have usually got promoted to sainthood anyway. Church interiors are generally crowded with the tall, colourful (or gaudy) statues of saints, set around like silent, passive friends, amongst whom ordinary people can sit, perhaps to draw comfort and inspiration for their own lives.

Crozon church's most famous feature is the reredos to the 10,000 martyrs, on the right-hand side of the main altar. This large and brightly coloured carving is supposed to depict the martyrdom of 10,000 Christian soldiers, who died for their faith

10   *The beach at Beg-Meil, Finistère*

11   *The church at Tronoën, Finistère, from the south (see overleaf)*

12   *The calvary at Tronoën – the oldest calvary in Brittany*

during the reign of the Emperor Hadrian. It has 12 panels of pictures in the centre and six panels of pictures on shutters either side. That they were done about the end of the fifteenth century, probably by two local artists, is all that is really known about them. Why they are here and their connection with Crozon is a mystery.

Opposite the reredos is a more recent memorial, a modern painting showing a girl with her head in Christ's lap, while listed below are the names of all those of Crozon Morgat who died during the war (1939–45), listing how they died and their ages. On a wall beside the chapel on the other side of the church is a list of names of those who died in the 1914–18 War, a tremendously large number for such a small place. But this is fairly typical of most Breton towns and villages.

If you have a car, and this is really a necessity on the Crozon peninsula unless you like long walks, you should do a grand tour, visiting the small isolated hamlet of Landévennec with its ruined abbey and museum, and the various points, such as the Pointe de la Chèvre (view over the Atlantic), Pointe des Espagnols (this was defended by a Spanish force against English and French combined); the Pointe de Dinan (shaped like a dog's head and with fantastic and colourful caves); and particularly the Pointe de Penhir.

Not far from the Pointe de Penhir is Camaret sur Mer (the name comes from the Breton word, *kamélet*), one of the most attractive of Brittany's fishing port/resorts. Whitewashed, grey slate-roofed houses climb the hills behind its peaceful harbour. Lobsters are the chief catch, but the fishermen now have to search for them farther afield than the coastal waters. Underwater fishing and sailing are the two most popular sea sports at Camaret; there are also regular boat services to Molène, Ouessant and Brest (via Le Fret).

The yachting harbour lies on the other side of a long esplanade on which stands a quaint little chapel and Vauban-fortified tower, entered by a wooden bridge across a moat. This holds the honour of having repulsed an Anglo-Dutch attack in 1694, when troops tried to make a landing here. Louis XIV, in recognition of Camaret's valour, had a medal struck to commemorate the occasion, and gave the town the title, *Custos Orae Amorocae* ('custodian of the Breton shore'). Also, and probably more popular, he excused the inhabitants from paying the detested hearth tax. The tower now houses a museum.

The chapel, picturesquely spelled Roc'h-am-a-dour, was burned down in 1527. Its bell tower was broken off in 1694 by an English cannon ball. It was also accidentally burned down in 1910, but was rebuilt again, keeping to its old style. Inside it is a truly nautical little chapel. Apart from the usual painted statues, there is also a sailing boat suspended from the central beam, a fleet of steamers in a glass case before the side altar, along with anchors, lifebelts and oars. A Pardon is held here on the first Sunday in September, following the blessing of the sea.

The walk to Pointe Penhir from Camaret is uphill and passes some menhirs arranged in three sides of a square. The Crozon peninsula was a prehistoric dwelling place, but unfortunately most of the old stones have disappeared, having been used for other buildings. The last few kilometres out to the end of the peninsula lie along a path through heather, the sea either side. From the farthest point you can see the left-hand shape of the coast, the Pointe de Dinan, and in the very distance, Europe's farthest point, the Pointe du Raz.

However, the best view of the sea and the Tas des Pois ('heap of peas') – a famous string of rocks – is from the platform to the right of the granite monument. From here, you can see the shape of the coast, Pointe du Toulinguet, Pointe St Mathieu, and in the dim distance, the island of Ouessant. The monument, incidentally, is dedicated to the Bretons of the Free French army, and was inaugurated by De Gaulle in 1951. A pilgrimage is held here each year by Bretons of the Resistance.

A walk to the Pointe du Toulinguet leads through pretty country but ends disappointingly in a military fort, which you are forbidden to enter.

The drive from Crozon eastwards and inland towards Châteaulin is a particularly pleasant one, through undulating countryside, past woodlands and fields and villages, complete as usual with church with tall towers and surrounded by an enormous churchyard. Although I was travelling in November, the gardens and churchyards were still crowded with flowers – even roses – on this beautifully warm and sunny day.

Then, first in the distance, but later on the left, loomed Ménez Hom, Brittany's highest mountain. From its top, which can be reached by car, there is the most splendid view of the entire Crozon peninsula, also of Cornouaille (the Pte du Van) on the left, and of the Brest Roadstead on the right.

Châteaulin, lying on the bend of the Aulne river, is one of the chief salmon-fishing centres in the Aulne valley. There is even a salmon on the town's coat of arms. Situated beside a railway line and with regular bus services, it makes a good excursion centre, being within easy reach of Pleyben and the Monts d'Arrée, as well as connecting with the Crozon peninsula and Quimper, capital of the Cornouaille.

Cornouaille

This old kingdom, later the medieval duchy of Cornouaille, the French Cornwall, once stretched far farther north and east of its capital, Quimper, than it does today.

But it is still a real old corner of Brittany, a country of Pardons and calvaries, and where you are more likely to see women wearing the traditional black dress and white coiffes – flat lace caps or miniature menhirs – than in any other part. Its seacoast is rocky and exciting. Its interior is flat and well-cultivated with field after field of vegetables or green pasture for grazing cows. You will see many little hamlets of grey or white stone houses with usually a white mist billowing gently in the distance.

Like the Abers, it has its quota of legends, the most famous one being about its king, the Roi Gradlon, who lived during the sixth century, when a town named Ys was the capital of Cornouaille.

This town, which was very beautiful, was protected from the

sea by a dyke. The king always carried the golden key which opened its lock about with him. Alas, this good man had a lovely but dissolute daughter, who had fallen in love with a young man who was really the devil in disguise. He begged her to steal the key from her father and open the gate. This she did, while he was sleeping, and the sea rushed into the town. Although the king woke in time, and mounted his horse, pulling his daughter up behind him, the angry waves followed. They would have swallowed him, too, had not a celestial voice ordered him to throw his daughter back behind him into the water.

The king obeyed with aching heart, and the sea withdrew. But the town still lay buried beneath its waves.

Gradlon chose Quimper for his new capital. The good St Corentin, its first bishop, became his guide and chief adviser. But his daughter, who was turned into a mermaid, and known as Maria Morgane, is still supposed to lure sailors to their death. According to tradition, the curse will only be broken and the city of Ys come back on the day that Mass is celebrated in one of the churches of the drowned city. However, to make things even more difficult, Ys is claimed to be in three different places – beyond the Baie des Trépassés, the Baie de Douarnenez and Pen Marc'h.

Quimper, lying in a pretty little valley, a town of towers and spires, is an attractive, almost elegant place, compared with most of Brittany's plain homespun towns. Its name means 'confluence' and comes from its two rivers, the Odet and Steir, which converge here.

The river Odet, which has been tamed to run neatly behind railings with pavements lined with trees either side, makes its sluggish, smelly, yet dignified way straight through the town. While the Steir, which cuts across the opposite way, is narrower, less formal, livelier, and has more character, especially when it splashes below the old jutting-out houses and turrets.

There are so many quaint narrow cobbled streets running up and down hills and over bridges that Quimper is a town just to wander through, especially the *vieux quartier*. But if possible choose a time when there is no traffic about. The lay part of the city, as opposed to the episcopal part, lies chiefly beyond the Place Terre au Duc.

St Corentin's cathedral (thirteenth to sixteenth centuries) lies in the episcopal area, its twin spires being the city's landmark. Although they only date from 1856, they blend in so well with the rest of the cathedral, that no one would have guessed that they had not been built earlier. To pay for their building the bishop asked the faithful of the diocese to pay one *sou* a year each for five years.

Before the cathedral stands the statue of a man on horseback, who, as you might guess, is King Gradlon. The street leading to the cathedral is named after him, while the square is called after his bishop.

The cathedral's façade with its large flamboyant portal, the high windows of its towers and openwork balconies, is very elegant, as is its interior, in spite of the fact that the thirteenth-century choir is out of line with the fifteenth-century nave. The fifteenth-century stained glass in the upper window is particularly fine. There is a little garden attached to the cathedral with lawns, flowerbeds and seats, and even a paddling pool and sandpit thoughtfully provided for children.

Quimper has some good museums, especially the Beaux Arts, which possesses Rubenses, Bouchers, Fragonards and Corots, amongst others. Quimper is also renowned for its pottery and you can visit a museum and working pottery if you wish. Quimper is probably most famous as being a centre of folklore: if you should happen to be there on the fourth Sunday in July you will find the whole town celebrating the Great Festival of Cornouaille, the biggest folklore festival in France.

Moreover, it is a grand centre for excursions and expeditions by bus, car or train, most of which do not entail much travelling time (though a popular drive in Cornouaille is that around the rocky, indented coast – approximately 320 km.).

Visit Locronan first, a little jewel of a town, set between forests on a steep hill. Its fine Renaissance square tells of wealthier days, when its inhabitants made their money from the manufacture of sailcloth. Taking into account all the places that manufactured it in Brittany, there must have been a great demand!

Locronan means 'holy place of Ronan' and refers to St Ronan, an Irish hermit, who lived in the wooded hills above the town. And it is to this place that the Petit Troműny (another word for Pardon) comes on a Sunday in July, rewalking St Ronan's everyday barefoot route. Every sixth year there is a Grand Troműny, which lasts a week, and in which many other villages take part.

Douarnenez is a large and busy fishing port (also seaside resort if you include Tréboul with it), lying either side of an estuary, and giving its name to the whole bay between the Crozon Peninsula and Cap Sizun. Cap Sizun, known as the Cap, incorporates the famous Pointe du Raz and the Pointe du Van, and is Europe's westernmost peninsula. Cap Sizun also contains a bird sanctuary, which can be visited between the 15th of March and the 31st of August (10 a.m. to noon and 2 p.m. to 6 p.m.; the conducted tour takes half an hour).

St Tugen (you will have to make a detour to visit it) has an interesting sixteenth-century chapel and a saint (his statue stands near to the high altar on the right), who was renowned for his bizarre habit of carrying a key that when touched by another key would drive away mad dogs!

Audierne is another attractive fishing port set picturesquely at the foot of a wooded hill round the mouth of the Goyen estuary. One of its fishing specialities is crayfish, delicately flavoured, which you might care to try.

After Plouzévet, which has an attractive thirteenth–fifteenth-century church, you are approaching the low-lying Penmarc'h peninsula, which, in contrast to the steep indented coastline of Cap Sizun opposite, sweeps round in a coveless 12-mile bay. The famous and very powerful Eckmühl lighthouse stands at the extreme end of the peninsula.

Strange to relate, the Penmarc'h peninsula was once one of the most prosperous parts of Brittany, when its inhabitants chiefly made their living by cod fishing. Then disaster followed disaster.

The cod deserted their coastal waters and a tidal wave wrought great destruction. Finally, during the anarchy produced by the religious wars a notorious brigand, named La Fontenelle, took advantage of the situation to attack this area. Many houses were destroyed and people killed. La Fontenelle loaded his booty on to ships and returned to his island, La Tristan, which he had captured, in the bay of Douarnenez.

Still, he got his deserts in the end. He was seized in 1602 (during reign of Henri IV), and was sentenced to be broken on the wheel, then to be publicly exposed until he died. But Penmarc'h never really recovered from all this.

Not far from the town of Penmarc'h is the calvary of Notre Dame du Tronoën, much weather-beaten because of its exposed position, but having the honour of being the oldest calvary in Brittany.

Pont l'Abbé, with its shady quays, situated at the head of an estuary, is the chief town of the Pays Bigouden, and is famous for its traditional costumes, particularly the tall white lace caps worn by the women. Apart from market gardening, one of the main industries is making little dolls dressed in the traditional costumes of the different French provinces. Its name Pont l'Abbé comes from the bridge built by the monks of Loctudy between the *étang* ('pool') and the harbour. From the little port of Loctudy you can take the boat up the river to Quimper.

In fact, the river trip starting from Quimper down the Odet is one of the most delightful excursions you can take from Quimper. The boat stops first at Bénodet, a very pretty and fashionable seaside resort and yachting harbour. Then if you want to, you can continue on to Loctudy, then the Glénan Isles, an archipelago of nine islets and home of a famous sailing school.

Local buses from Quimper (bus station in the Boulevard de Kerguelen) go to the Monts d'Arrée and the Montagnes Noires, also to places along the Cornouaille coast. I took one via Audierne to the Pointe du Raz.

The journey there ended rather disappointingly in a car park. Ahead and all around lay billowing mist. I could only just distinguish the long line of buildings and the word 'café' through the fog.

'Voilà l'Atlantique. Next stop America,' said the driver. I was his only passenger – the only person probably mad enough to come in November. Dismounting, shivering and turning up his coat collar, he made quickly for the café and a warm drink.

In spite of my frustration, I was determined to see more of this famous headland, and made my way stumbling towards the edge of the grass, not sure what lay beyond, and hoping that I wouldn't fall over the cliffs.

However, my luck was in. As I walked, so the large pile of rocks before me gradually extended itself into the beginning of a spur and the mist rolled slowly backwards rather like a curtain lifting to reveal the most wonderful views of headlands, high cliffs and foaming water below.

A fisherman made his way along the spur of rock to a pool, just out of sight. Concluding that it was now safe enough I followed him forward over the rocks and might, had there been time, have reached the end of the spur. But perhaps I should add that there are guides, whose office is near the café, who will take parties along the Pointe du Raz unless there is a mist or it is very windy. It is not unknown for people to be blown off the Pointe in a high wind.

Far out at sea and beyond the lighthouse lies the island of Sein, which can be reached by boat from the mainland. It is low and bare with no trees or bushes, but vegetables, especially potatoes, and barley are grown. The houses are tiny and lie along narrow streets. Not surprisingly, the inhabitants lived here in complete isolation until the eighteenth century, when they were converted to Christianity by the Jesuit fathers.

Up to then they were greatly feared by the people living on the mainland because of their habit of looting wrecks, of which there were usually plenty. Today, they are more renowned for their skill at life-saving, although they do still obtain benefits from shipwrecks off their coast. Much of the furniture in their houses is made from shipwrecks. The lighthouse on the island was built in 1881 to warn ships off this dangerous area.

The men, mostly sailors and lobster fishermen, are very independent. In June 1940 they all put to sea and joined the Free French Army in England. In 1946 they were awarded the Liberation Cross by General de Gaulle for their valour.

The Baie des Trépassés, an innocent-looking stretch of sand to the right of the Pointe du Raz, was supposed to have got its name, Bay of the Dead, from the number of people washed up in it after being drowned off this coast. Although according to another theory it is because, according to ancient tradition, this was the bay from which the corpses of druids were taken to the island of Sein for burial.

Another place which can be visited not far from Quimper is Concarneau, a large fishing port and lively sea resort, with the added attraction of a wonderful old walled town, the Ville Clos.

This is approached from the quay by crossing two bridges which pass under a gateway into a fortified courtyard laid out with flowers. From here, if you like, you can enter a white gate beside the entrance (a charge is made) and walk round part of the ramparts, which give a good view of the harbour and fishing port.

Another gateway leads from the courtyard below into the Rue Vauban, passing the Musée de la Pêche, which is installed in what was once part of the town's fortications. Here you can learn how fishing techniques developed and the history of the town.

Like other such places, Concarneau is just pleasant to wander through, up and down its narrow cobbled streets, and peering through the occasional archways, which lead on to tiny quays and out at the sea beyond.

In the centre square is a green crocodile swallowing a fish holding aloft a lantern, doing duty both as a fountain and a light. Not far from here an arrow indicates another viewpoint and another part of the ramparts, from which to watch the yachts and fishing boats in the bay and Atlantic beyond.

According to a plaque on the wall nothing has changed here since Louis xiv's time, when Vauban improved and added to its fortifications. Before that, however, Concarneau lived through some stirring times.

Some sort of fortress, although primitive, has existed on this island rock since about the ninth century, when it was used by the fishermen and people living round about as an easily-defended place of refuge. By the thirteenth century it was surrounded by a stone wall and reckoned to be one of the strongest fortified places in Brittany. During the War of Succession, it was held for Montfort and was occupied by an English garrison for 30 years. In 1373 it stood up to two assaults by Du Guesclin, but was conquered by the third in 1378. It was reconstructed and improved by two dukes of Brittany, Peter II and François II. During the Wars of Religion it was mostly held by the Catholic Leaguers, except for a short time when, after it had been taken by surprise, it was held by a group of Huguenots from Morbihan. Later, royalist troops assaulted and seized it for Louis XIII and France. Louis XIV had his military architect, Vauban, turn it into part of France's seaboard defences. Today, its mild climate and tranquil atmosphere have turned it into a peaceful haven suitable for harbouring the sick and recuperating. I noticed two hospitals within its sturdy walls.

After visiting the Ville Clos, you can stroll round the fishing harbour, along the Pierre Guéguin and the Quai Carnot. Concarneau is one of the most important fishing harbours in France – tunny fish, sardines, herrings, shrimps, etc. – and on the last Sunday but one in August, the Fête of the Filets Bleus ('blue nets'), one of the oldest of Brittany's folklore festivals, is held here.

If you walk the other way you will pass the Quai de Croix, the lighthouse and the fifteenth-century chapel of Notre Dame de Bon Secours and eventually reach the Plage des Petits Sables Blancs, and the Plage des Grands Sables Blancs.

La Forêt Fousenant, a small peaceful village, surrounded by orchards – the best Breton cider is produced here – lies farther along and inland at the head of a creek. Cap Coz has lovely sandy beaches, good bathing and a sailing school. Beg Meil, a high-class resort, now very popular with the English, can also be reached by boat from Concarneau, as can the Glénan Islands.

The Pointe du Cabellou (a good viewing-point of the coastline) lies the opposite way, as do Port Raguenès Plage, Port Manech (an unspoilt little fishing port), Pont-Aven (picturesquely set where the Aven meets the estuary, beloved by the Impressionists, especially Gaugin, and still much favoured by artists), Riec-sur-Belon (famous for its succulent oysters) and Le Pouldu (also a favourite haunt of Gauguin).

Quimperlé, a small town situated at the junction of the Isole and Ellé rivers, connected by rail and road with Quimper and Vannes (Morbihan), and within easy reach of the Argoat and most of the south coast seaside resorts, makes a good centre for excursions.

5. Morbihan

The Morbihan, which is situated in the centre and south of Brittany, takes its name from the Gulf of Morbihan (which means 'little sea'). Winters are mild along its coast, which is less indented than the north and west. Fishing is an important industry, especially for sardines and tunny, and oysters are bred in the Gulf. As the land is not very fertile farming is chiefly confined to cattle-rearing and dairy production, and orchards for cider apples. The Morbihan is something of a rural backwater and is considered a backward area of France. Breton is still spoken in its western part.

Inland Area

The village of Le Faouët, not far from Quimperlé, lies on the edge of the Montagnes Noires. But its vast sixteenth-century market-place built out of wood and roofed with tiles makes it seem more like a town. The surrounding country is attractive and the two nearby chapels of Ste Barbe and St Fiacre are worth seeing.

Ste Barbe (St Barbara) is a very popular Breton saint, and quite a busy bee. Not only is she the patron saint of all to do with fire, buildings and stone masons, but also of artillerymen and grave-diggers.

Ste Barbe is really a cluster of buildings, which stand on a wooded hillside looking over the Ellé river, for it incorporates an inn, a small bell tower in which pilgrims can toll to attract heaven's blessed attention, as well as the small fifteenth-century

Gothic chapel (this possesses some delicately-carved panels and fine Renaissance stained-glass windows) and a monumental classical stone staircase which leads to an upper terrace. From here a balustraded bridge takes you to a tiny oratory, St Michel, perched on a rock above. According to local tradition, Ste Barbe's chapel was built by a local landowner in gratitude for being saved from being crushed by a rock which had been dislodged by lightning.

Pearly-grey St Fiacre, also fifteenth-century, and more of a church than a chapel, is dedicated to the patron saint of gardeners. Its best features are its triple tower and its superb lace-like carved wooden rood screen, decorated on the nave side with the statues of the archangel Gabriel, the Virgin, St John and Adam and Eve. The figures on the chancel side show various sins, such as theft, lust, drunkenness and laziness and are quite extraordinary and fascinating to look at.

St Fiacre has a curious connection with Kernascléden, about 21 km. to the east. Although its church was consecrated in 1453, about 30 years before St Fiacre, there is a legend that they were built by the same workmen, who were somehow conveyed through time and space from one site to the other by angels.

This Breton church is famous for the perfection of the detail of its workmanship. Its façade, with its gable and rose window surmounted by a slender steeple, has elegance and a purity of line. Inside are some remarkable fifteenth-century frescoes (restored), portraying scenes from the life of Christ and the Virgin. For those who like the lurid, there is a *danse macabre* in the south transept giving a most fantastic representation of Hell and showing a variety of tortures.

Busy Pontivy, situated where the river Blavet is joined by the Nantes–Brest canal, is the principal market town of central Brittany. Its name comes from the bridge built by the monks of Ivy, whose name in turn came from an early Celtic bishop. The town is also linked with the ancient and noble family of de Rohan, one of whose dukes, Jean II, built its castle (only recently restored) in 1485.

Pontivy is an intriguing mixture of centuries. Its Flamboyant Gothic church and Place des Martyrs, old houses and surrounding narrow streets with names such as Rue du Fil (Yarn Street) and Rue de Perroquet (Topgallant Street), recall the Middle Ages, when sailcloth was one of Brittany's chief productions. While the Place d'Armes, Avenue Napoléon, and straight streets lined with austere buildings recall the newer, military spirit of the First Empire.

During the Napoleonic wars, when Britain still ruled the seas, Napoleon decided to build a canal across Brittany, linking Brest with Nantes. As Pontivy lies about halfway between, it seemed a good idea to make it the strategic and military centre of a province of uncertain loyalty. Roads, barracks, a Town Hall, a court and school as well as the canal (now no longer used above Pontivy), were all constructed. The town even changed its name to Napoléonville. However, after the fall of his empire building stopped and, except for a period during the time of Napoleon III, the name Napoléonville was dropped; Pontivy returned to its role of provincial town. Even so, the layout of its wide streets, often named after Napoleonic battles, recalls more heroic times. If its buildings are not particularly noble, then the gorgeous flowers and shrubs planted round about are compensation.

Pontivy, linking as it does with the Montagne Noires and places of interest such as Vannes, Josselin and the Lac de Guerlédan, makes a good excursion centre.

The long lake of Guerlédan, one of the sights of inland Brittany, is really in Côtes-du-Nord, but I have put it in this Morbihan chapter because it is more easily approached from there. This magnificent stretch of water is a reservoir made from the abandoned canal which once flowed through the deep gorge of the Blavet river.

The large village of Mer-de-Bretagne, set amidst trees, is a good place to start on the 40-km. tour of the lake. There is a good panorama of the big dam and the canal linking Nantes to Mer-de-Bretagne via Pontivy, if you leave the village on the D18 and walk or drive about 2 km.

You will then have to return to Mur-en-Bretagne to start the grand tour of the lake from the south. You take the D35 on the right and after the canal turn right on to the D31.

At St Aignan there is a pretty little church and if you make another detour about one kilometre down to the lake, you will find another good viewing point looking out over the dam.

Back on the road again, you will eventually come to the Quénécan forest, undulating and green. The surrounding hills, waters and trees form a landscape which is known as the Suisse Bretonne. However, the forest, once much larger, has been gradually eroded, so that a lot of it now is just scrubland and heath. Most of the oak and beech groves lie around the Forges des Salles.

This is an attractive leafy hamlet which got its name from the iron ore which was smelted here until the beginning of the last century. The ruined castle, now converted into a farmhouse, also lies in this valley. Not far from here lies another 'has been', a roofless overgrown ruin, which was once the twelfth-century Abbey of Bon Repos and, in its heyday, was under the charge of Cardinal Mazarin.

You should not miss going up the gorges of the Daoulas by the D44. Here the river cuts deep and swift through rocks to join the Blavet. The narrow, winding, steep-sided valleys are covered in gorse, broom, heather and foxgloves, with birch trees growing gracefully near the water's edge.

You join the N164 about 1½ km. along the valley on the left and continue about five km. to Keriven, where there is a very good view of the lake, then rejoin the N164 at Caurel. You can now return to Mur-en-Bretagne by the N167, or continue along the N164*bis*, then turn up the D63 to the narrow, rocky and wooded Poulancre gorges and St Gilles du Vieux Marché.

Josselin, about 34 km. to the east of Pontivy is one of Brittany's loveliest medieval towns. Its château is a must for every visitor to the province.

You should see it first from the bridge over the Oust, coming from the direction of Malestroit. It is a truly fairytale castle, with strong walls and tall pointed towers, all seeming to grow straight out of the rocks, proudly mirrored in the dark waters below.

You will have to climb steps and follow passages round to its entrance on the other side. Josselin, still owned by the de Rohans, is a real stately home. Its gardens lead into an inner court and the long, low Gothic façade, a masterpiece of Flamboyant carving, makes strong contrast with the grim but picturesque defences outside. Inside are stone walls and heavy beamed ceilings, which underwent considerable restoration at the end of the last century.

The first château was built here in the year 1000 by the Viscount de Porhoët and was finished by his son, Josselin, who gave his name both to the castle and to the town which grew up round it.

The castle played an important part during the War of Succession and the Hundred Years' War. By the middle of the fourteenth century it had already been razed and rebuilt. It then belonged to the King of France and had as its captain Jean de Beaumanoir, who was also Marshal of Brittany for Charles de Blois. Nearby Ploërmel (a town now famous for its pig markets) was held by John Bramborough for Montfort, who was supported by the King of England.

The two garrisons ravaged the countryside. Although they had frequent encounters, neither side could ever call itself victorious. Eventually, to end this stalemate, Beaumanoir sent the English captain a challenge, which was accepted. A battle between 30 picked men would take place. The result would mean the defeat and withdrawal of one of them.

So, on 27 March 1351, a fight between Ploërmel and Josselin took place at Mi Voie (a stone pyramid now marks the spot). On Beaumanoir's side were 30 Bretons; on Bramborough's side, 20 Englishmen, six German mercenaries, and four Bretons. The battle was fought with lances, swords, daggers and maces.

The fight was hard and bitter. At one stage, when the wounded Beaumanoir called for water, Geoffrey de Blois shouted to his wounded leader, 'Drink your blood, Beaumanoir; that will quench your thirst.' Victory was decided when Gillaume de Montauban

13 Pardon *in the rain at Bénodet*

mounted his horse and overthrew seven of the English champions. Those remaining were forced to surrender. Most of the combatants were killed or seriously wounded, Bramborough himself being among the slain.

Amongst the owners of Josselin the most famous was Olivier de Clisson, who succeeded Du Guesclin as Constable of France, and who married Marguerite of Rohan, the widow of Beaumanoir. He strengthened the castle's fortifications, building eight towers and a great keep. He died here in 1407.

François II of Brittany seized Josselin in 1488 and to punish its owner, Jean II de Rohan, for having sided with the French king, he had it dismantled. However, when his daughter became Queen of France she was obliged to compensate him for this by helping him rebuild it. Because of this you will often see the letter 'A' among the castle's decorations : a token of the family's gratitude, and also a proof of their Breton loyalty. The dukes of Rohan transformed the castle into a worthy noble seat during the sixteenth century, when it became a masterpiece of Renaissance art, well justifying the family's motto, 'I cannot be a king; I scorn to be a prince; I am a Rohan'. Quite a wise one as it turned out, for they are still there, while France's royal family has long since relinquished its throne.

One of the Rohans, Henri, was a leader of the Huguenots, arch-enemies of Richelieu. So, in 1629, during the reign of Louis XIII, the Cardinal saw to it that its great keep and four of its towers were demolished. Its exterior today is much as it was then.

To take a stroll round Josselin, wandering through its cobbled streets and up and down stairways, is like turning the pages of a history book. Many street names recall important happenings, such as the Rue des Trente (Street of the 30), or people, like Rue Olivier de Clisson.

Its basilica of Notre-Dame-du-Roncier (Our Lady of the bramble field) got its name from an old legend. About 808 a workman discovered a statue of the Virgin Mary hidden under some brambles. He took it home, but the statue disappeared to be found later in the field. He took it home again. Again it disappeared, but was found in the same place. This continued until he got the

14 The standing stones at Carnac, Morbihan

message. The Virgin wanted a sanctuary built on the site where he'd found her. So this was done.

The present basilica was founded about the fourteenth century, but has been restored and rebuilt many times. Its name only dates from the fifteenth century. The old statue of the Virgin was burned in 1793 during the Revolution, but although only a fragment remains, this is enough for the pilgrims who come here on Pardon day. Olivier de Clisson, who did much to improve the church, is buried there, as is his wife, Marguerite de Rohan, in the mausoleum in the chapel to the right of the chancel.

Not far from Josselin is the famous Guéhenno calvary. Built in 1550 (since restored) it shows many of the characteristics of the parish enclosures of Finistère. The ossuary behind has been transformed into Christ's tomb, guarded by soldiers: above it stands the triumphant risen Christ.

Vannes and the Morbihan Gulf

Vannes, relaxed, friendly yet dignified, lying on the Morbihan Gulf, is a city of old walls, gardens and flowers. It is the smallest and also has the honour of being the first and last of Brittany's capitals.

For Vannes had its own independent counts as early as the sixth century, and it was here that Nominoé, as Count of Vannes, declared himself ruler of Brittany. Centuries later, in 1532, the Council, meeting at Vannes, proclaimed the perpetual union of the county and duchy of Brittany with the kingdom and crown of France.

The best place to start a tour of the city is from the helpful Syndicat d'Initiative, beside the Hôtel de Limur (this has a magnificent staircase and garden) in the Rue Thiers, just outside where the ramparts of the old town once stood.

This leads up to the Town Hall Square, where stands the mounted statue of Arthur Richemont, born in nearby Suscino in 1393, Duke of Brittany, a Constable of France, and who also had the distinction of fighting with Jeanne d'Arc. The Town Hall behind, formal and Renaissance in style, was built at the end of the last century.

If you leave the square by the Rue Emile Burgault, you will find yourself in the old part of the city. The Place Henri IV is surrounded by timbered fifteenth- and sixteenth-century houses, between the rooftops of which looms the Romanesque tower of the cathedral, St Pierre.

St Pierre, which was built between the thirteenth and nineteenth centuries, is difficult to see properly outside and is disappointing within. Better to visit the round Renaissance chapel, built by Canon Danielo when under the influence of the classical monuments he had seen in Italy, at the beginning of the sixteenth century. This is in the Rue des Chanoines, which skirts the north side of the cathedral.

To the right of the cathedral is the Rue St Guenhaël, named after a Celtic saint and bordered with medieval shops. If you take this back to the Place Henri IV, then the Halles, you should come out into the Place des Lices.

Here, at the top on the left, is the fifteenth-century house of Vannes and his wife, the city's mascot. Two merry faces stick out from a wooden beam. Exactly who they are is still a mystery. Most probably, they once lived here, as it was sometimes the custom for medieval people to have themselves carved on their houses. According to old records, there was a family in the town who took the name of Vannes as a surname. One was a coiner, another was a bishop, another was president of the duke's exchequer, yet another was a captain in Duke Jean V's bowmen. The man's head may refer to any or none of these.

Almost opposite stands the fifteenth-century Château Gaillard, once the residence of Bishop Jean de Malestroit, then a meeting place for Brittany's refugee parliament, which was exiled from Rennes by Louis XIV after revolting against the Stamp Act in 1675. Times change. Now the tower staircase leads to a room devoted to the prehistoric treasures found in the Carnac region, one of the best museums of its kind in Brittany. There is also a Natural Science museum here.

In nearby Valencia square is an interesting old house, which contains the death chamber of St Vincent Ferrier, now transformed into a chapel (his tomb and relics are in the round chapel of the cathedral).

Vincent Ferrier was born in Valencia, Spain, and came to Vannes in 1419, where he preached and later died. Historically he is quite an important figure, as it was largely due to his efforts that the schism which divided the papacy in the fourteenth century was healed. He was canonized in 1455.

Although St Vincent only spent two years in Brittany he had an important evangelizing effect, using a combination of homely stories and rhetoric to put across his message. From him dates the religious fervour which led to the establishment of so many calvaries, crosses, churches, chapels and Pardons, and was maintained by those two great seventeenth-century missionaries, Le Nobletz and Maunoir.

Although the old part of Vannes is interesting to wander round, particularly if you know a little of its history, in my view the best part of the city lies on the east and south sides. Here medieval ramparts, interspersed with towers, blend well with the eighteenth-century formal gardens, especially when floodlit.

If you take the Rue St Guenhaël, beyond the cathedral, you will come out to the fourteenth/fifteenth-century Porte Prison. Next turn right down Rue Alexandre le Pontois, which eventually leads into the Place Gambetta and the harbour.

You will first pass the gardens of the Préfecture, then Les Ramparts, with its attractive flower beds (on the right) and the garden of the Garenne (on the left). Here you will see a very fine cenotaph to the two world wars. There is also a commemorative plate in memory of those who were shot here for the part they played in the Quiberon landing. These 22 were the most important ones and included the Bishop of Dol. They were imprisoned in the nearby sturdy granite Constable Tower, built during the War of Succession, after Vannes had been besieged four times.

The garden once belonged to Jean IV, Duke of Brittany, who built the Château d'Ermine on what was then reclaimed marshland. The castle got its name from the emblem of Breton chivalry, the Order of the Ermine, which Jean IV founded. However, the present Château Hermine with its grand formal façade was rebuilt in 1800 for a Vanetoise trader, replacing the old residence of the Duke of Vannes.

More mundane, but very picturesque, are the old washing places that border the stream beyond the walls and garden. Here the washerwomen of long ago chattered and clattered at their humdrum but necessary task.

Beyond the southern Porte St Vincent is the port of Vannes, a wide quay with a broad canal, but some distance from the open waters of the Morbihan. It is not now used as it is silted up. Even the little motor boats which make trips to the Morbihan islands start from Conleau, about 5 km. away.

You will notice many CTM (Compagnie de Transports du Morbihan) bus stops around Vannes from which you can catch a bus to the Conleau peninsula. Once there, you walk through a wood to a village and down to a small jetty. The boats are supposed to link up with the buses, and are fairly frequent in the season.

You can, of course, drive round the shores of the gulf by car: westwards to visit Auray and Locmariaquer, or eastwards visiting the Rhuys peninsula (the better trip). But the boat journey across the gulf makes the more interesting expedition.

The Morbihan, which came about by a comparatively recent re-settling of this part of the coast, is about 19 km. wide and 16 long. There are innumerable little islands – about 365 – of which only 40 are occupied. They are low, flat wooded and often hidden by mist. At high tide many of them look as if they are just floating above the water, while some of them do actually disappear. At low tide, which seems more frequent, they resemble long low sandbanks. The area is famous for its sunsets and beautiful light effects. Although peaceful, much boating activity takes place – fishing, sailing, pleasure craft and regattas in summer – on this wide stretch of inland sea.

If you take the vedette from Vannes round the gulf, you can visit the two main islands, Arz and Moines, and Port Navalo and

Locmariaquer, perhaps stopping at one of these places and catching another boat later.

In a way, I preferred the little island of Arz (about three kilometres long) to the larger Ile aux Moines, which is more popular, and therefore gets very crowded in season. Arz's tiny village, Gréavet, is about two kilometres from the landing stage, but you can arrange transport to take you there if you don't feel like walking.

The Ile aux Moines (monks), about six kilometres long, was originally known as 'Izenah' in Breton. The monks, who were from Redon, were given it by Erispoe, a Breton 'king' about A.D. 854. The monks have now departed, but their memory still lingers on in their name.

There are now about 750 people living there, who mostly make their living from the sea – fishing, oyster-culture, boats for transport and pleasure, and, of course, tourism. About a century ago, the population was much larger, but many families left, although some people have returned to retire here. Also, quite a number of people live here for part of the year, particularly in July and August, when the number of inhabitants rises to about 5,000. So should you decide to spend a holiday here, come in spring at daffodil time, or in autumn, when the broom is out.

Moines boasts some prehistoric megaliths, as does Arz, but they are not easy to find. One kilometre to the south of Bourg is the Kergonan Cromlech, one of the largest in France, and further along the same road is the Boglieux dolmen, near a magnificent view of the gulf. To the north of the town is a calvary, looking towards the Rhuys peninsula. There are other dolmens and menhirs to be seen, but the megaliths mentioned are the most famous.

Moines has some good hotels, restaurants and cafés, and has regular boat services and car ferries to the mainland. There are also a number of local festivals. Sailing, water-skiing, walking and sunbathing are the main activities. Its pretty little woods have the most evocative names. Bois des Soupirs ('wood of sighs'),

Bois d'Amour ('wood of love') and Bois des Regrets ('wood of regrets').

Arzon-Port Navalo, a fairly busy seaside resort with harbours and lovely sandy beaches, is situated on the Rhuys peninsula. This attractive region, on the eastern arm of the Gulf of Morbihan, has some small but endearing resorts, and is just now coming into its own. The climate is mild – mimosa, palm and fig trees flourish – and there are numerous beaches and many small harbours. It is warm and particularly attractive in May. Also, it is the only region in which Breton wine is produced (you can't now count that produced in the Loire Atlantique). This is cheap, rough and highly intoxicating, and may be the reason why the Morbihan has the highest rate of alcoholism in France.

Sarzeau is its capital and commercial centre. St Gildas du Rhuys has a particularly wide and beautiful beach, Les Govelins, also an old Romanesque church with a remarkable chancel. Among its treasures are the arms, legs and head of St Gildas, who founded the monastery, which gave its name to the town. Peter Abelard spent an unhappy period here during the twelfth century and was eventually obliged to escape through a secret passage after vain attempts to control the hostile and disorderly monks.

There is also Le Tour-du-Parc, which gets its name from the fact that noblemen who lived at Suscino near by used to make a tour round this area on horseback. Perhaps I should mention that Suscino (a corruption of *Souci n'y ot*) was a château built in 1218 and used by the dukes of Brittany as a summer abode intended for pleasure. In fact, it had quite a hectic time. It changed hands several times during the Wars of Succession, was captured by Du Guesclin, fortified by Mercoeur during the Wars of Religion and was occupied by the chouans and émigrés for a short time in 1795. It was later sold and partly demolished, its stones used for building. Today, its remaining towers and thick stone walls hide an interior as bare and melancholy as the surrounding countryside.

Locmariaquer, which is situated on the smaller western peninsula opposite the Rhuys peninsula, is a fishing village and pleasant family seaside resort. It is chiefly renowned for the Dolmen Mané

Lud and the great menhir (broken into five pieces weighing about 350 tons each, it is the biggest in France) and the Merchant Table Dolmen (three flat tables with 17 supports) near by.

The tumulus of Gavrinis, situated on the island of Gavrinis, at the mouth of the Gulf of Morbihan, can be reached by boat from Larmor Baden to its north (which can be reached by bus from Vannes), but only on certain days. Here in a lovely setting of gorse lies a Celtic king in his tomb, 25 feet high and 100 yards round. You can go inside and from on top there is a good view of the Gulf.

Vannes, situated so near the Gulf, with its boat, train and bus services, and within easy driving distance of many interesting places, makes an excellent centre for excursions.

However, if you are contemplating buses, BEWARE, for there are at least three companies running bus services here and they use different stopping places. C.T.M. does the trips to the Morbihan; Tomine to Josselin, and Drouin Fr. to Quiberon, Carnac and Auray. The best thing to do is to inquire at the Renseignements at Vannes railway station, or at the Syndicat d'Initiative in the Rue de Thiers, and find out *exactly* where the bus you want to use stops.

Auray, Carnac and the Quiberon Peninsula

You can visit Auray by boat across the gulf and up the Loch river, as well as by bus from Vannes. This old town, about 17 km. west of Vannes, also has its store of medieval houses, along with a flourishing and busy port. The oyster beds you will see along its estuary are among the largest in France. A good view of the port and river is to be had from the Loch promenade.

It is easy to pass through Auray, missing the best bits, for its most attractive part is hidden away. So leave the car or bus and explore it further on foot.

Take the steep narrow street from the busy Place de la République down the hillside to the long low bridge crossing the river. Downstream is a port for fishing boats and beyond the broad stone quay is the ancient quarter of St Goustan. Here alleyways and steps climb and twist in and out between a jumble of fifteenth- and sixteenth-century houses. Americans may be interested to know that Benjamin Franklin landed at this quayside while evading the British warships in 1776, when he was seeking aid from the French for the colonists in revolt. The house where he stayed bears a tablet.

Auray has played an important part in Breton history. While here, you can make an interesting 16-kilometre expedition to the Carthusian convent of Auray, the Champ des Martyrs and Ste Anne Auray.

The Carthusian convent, La Chartreuse, lies on the N168 along the Avenue du Général de Gaulle, and is about two kilometres to the north of Auray.

It was near here that the battle which ended the War of Succession was fought in 1364, and where Charles de Blois was killed. Although his death was necessary to John Montfort, the latter was greatly distressed when his body was picked up from the battlefield. He had him buried with great magnificence near Guincamp, and founded a chapel and collegiate church on the battlefield which later became a Carthusian monastery. Today it is a place where the Sisters of Sagesse devote themselves to the care of the young deaf and dumb.

The convent also contains a chapel, built during the restoration in 1823, which contains a mausoleum holding the bones and skulls of the 350 exiles and chouans who were shot in the nearby Champ des Martyrs after the ill-fated Quiberon landing. You can visit the actual enclosure in which they were shot. There is also a small expiatory chapel, built in 1828, near by.

Ste Anne Auray lies beyond the Champ des Martyrs and the Kerso bog on which the battle of Auray was fought (Charles's bad position was the chief reason why he lost) on the D120. Then you turn right on to the D19.

It is only a little place, yet it attracts more people to it in a year than probably anywhere else in Brittany. The reason for this is that it is the most popular place of pilgrimage. The first Pardon takes place on March 7th. Then from Easter until October parishes from all over the province have a jaunt here, partly religious and partly to celebrate (they have a very fine banquet in her honour).

This is the story behind it. In 1623 Ste Anne, mother of the Virgin Mary, appeared to a peasant named Yves Nicolazic, and commanded him to rebuild a chapel dedicated to her, which she claimed had stood in a field 924 years earlier. This was never proved and was unlikely anyway; nevertheless, Yves did find a statue of the saint while digging in the field on 7 March 1625. Since then a Pardon has taken place here every year on that date, along with the local ones and the greatest Pardon of all Brittany on the 26th of July, which is the feast day of Ste Anne, the province's patron saint.

Ste Anne's statue stands in the nineteenth-century Renaissance-style basilica in Ste Anne Auray (the original one was burned during the Revolution). Part of the original face was saved and this has been set in the base. The chapel walls are covered in votive offerings, some dating from the seventeenth century. The fountain in the square, surmounted by a statue of Ste Anne and supposedly miraculous, is rather lovely.

Carnac, which lies about 13 km. to the south-west of Auray, is the district *par excellence* of megaliths and pre-history. Several thousand stones cover this area, the most famous and easily reached being those of Ménec. This alignment lies along the D196, off the main road, just outside Carnac Ville. You can view them and the Tumulus St Michel (about three kilometres) by car, or better still, walk.

You come across the Ménec alignment suddenly and unexpectedly, behind a farmhouse and haystack, an amazing sight of upended boulders, all shapes and sizes – the tallest is 12 feet high – arranged in rows beside the roadside. Altogether there are 1,009 of these menhirs here. Their exact purpose and how and when they were constructed is still a matter of controversy.

If you have a car, the time and the inclination, you can continue along the D196 to pass the alignments of Kermario, also those of Kerlescan (D186) and the Tumulus of Moustoir and finish off at the Tumulus of St Michel (D119) on the outskirts of Carnac Ville.

If you are walking you will find that the road which runs alongside them eventually forks and you take the D119 back towards Carnac Ville. There can be no mistaking the Tumulus of St Michel, whose hill is on the left, for you will see it from afar. Various little lanes lead up to it, but if you continue you will reach a crossroads, and you should turn left up the Rue du Tumulus.

From the top of this mound there is a wonderful view of the fields, woods and houses of the surrounding countryside, especially the Quiberon peninsula beyond and its coastline. The table of orientation, set up by the Touring Club de France, tells where everything is. There is also a little chapel (locked) to St Michel, and a small calvary on the mount.

The tumulus, about 120 yards long and 40 feet wide, is a prehistoric tomb and its mound of earth and stones covers several burial chambers which can be explored – the entrance is through the iron door, under a porch of leaves, opposite the Hôtel du Tumulus. You have to apply at the hotel for a guide.

There are, of course, other alignments and groups of menhirs to view. Locmariaquer, which I have mentioned earlier, is only about 25 km. away, but the ones I have spoken of are the main ones to see.

A visit to the little museum in Carnac Ville is a must for anyone interested in archaeology, and it will certainly enrich your visit to the megaliths. If you should find it closed, you can call on its *gardien,* M. Jacq, who lives near by at 10 Rue du Goh Lore, who will open it for you.

The Museum is called the Musée Archéologique James Miln–Zacharie Le Rouzic. James Miln was a Scot who, after spending much of his life in China and India, returned to Europe when he was about 50. When he visited Carnac in Brittany about 1873, he was completely fascinated by the strange grandiose stone dolmens, menhirs, cromlechs and tumuli. Also, the rocky countryside reminded him of his native Scotland.

However, it was the Roman remains he stumbled on while out

walking which were to take up most of his attention. As he was a free agent, and sufficiently well off to indulge his interests, it wasn't long before he obtained the peasant-owner's permission to dig up his land. He then started on what was to be his life's work, the uncovering of a Gallo-Roman site with local assistance. His methods were unscientific and he must have dislodged a large number of objects without first measuring their position, doing considerable archaeological damage. Still he was first in that particular field, and one learns by the mistakes of others. And James Miln was certainly well-meaning. He kept a journal of his observations and published a work. Carnac became his home and he toured the whole area. The bedroom which he had rented in the Hotel Lautram soon became an overcrowded depository of finds; he was starting to think about acquiring somewhere more permanent to put them in when he unexpectedly died while in Edinburgh in 1881.

Fortunately, his brother Robert came to the rescue, and as James Miln had often stated he wanted to leave his collection to Carnac, he built at his own expense a place to house it. From then onwards there was a museum open to the public.

The other half of the museum's name belongs to Zacharie Le Rouzic, who was born at Carnac in 1864, the ninth child of a weaver. After leaving school at ten, he was taken on by James Miln to help him in his research and carry his equipment. Although he was not more than 17 at the time of his master's death, Robert Miln appointed him the museum's guardian under the direction of the mayor.

Like James Miln before him, he devoted his life to the cause of archaeology. Unlike his former master though, he was more interested in the ancient stones – which he believed belonged to a much earlier period than previously supposed – and their meaning, than the Gallo-Roman remains. He also had a more scientific approach and tried to classify the periods of the finds. Archaeologists of all nationalities were attracted to Carnac. So, as guardian, conservator and archaeologist, it was only just that his name be added to the museum's title.

Carnac is not only renowned for its megaliths. There is also its church of St Cornély, patron saint of horned cattle, whose Pardon is held in September. On the day of the fair, the priest blesses the cattle at the Saint's fountain. Then there is Carnac Plage, a gently sloping shore which is one of the finest and most popular beaches along the south coast of Brittany.

Carnac Ville and Carnac Plage were two villages which have expanded and joined together. You can drive to Carnac Plage from Carnac Ville down the Avenue du Salins, passing the Marais Salants, square pools of water, then down and round into the Avenue des Druides.

All roads to the right of this lead on to the long Grande Plage, bordered by villas, cafés, hotels, and pine trees. This rather formal seaside resort, much favoured by the English, has everything necessary for conventional holidays – amusement arcades, discothèques, riding, tennis, sailing, miniature golf, even a zoo. All this, with the menhir land behind, qualifies it to be called 'Stonehenge-on-Sea'.

The Quiberon peninsula, lying to the south-west, is often referred to as an island, because that is what it once was. Now it is connected to the mainland by a long, low, narrow sand bar, with pine trees pinning it down into the dunes. Its most attractive part is the Côte Sauvage, which faces towards the Atlantic. But it is on the east side, protected by that great gulf, the Bay of Quiberon, and in the south that you will find the resorts.

Quiberon, situated at its southern end, is the best place to stay, as not only does it have the largest beach, but it is from here that excursions can be made. Then it is blessed with a very good climate, which it owes to its position, its refreshing sea breezes and the fields of seaweed surrounding it. A luxurious sanatorium has been established there, where seawater cures are used to treat a variety of physical and nervous diseases, especially victims of road accidents.

The name Kerberoen goes back to the Breton emigrations of the sixth century, but excavations show that this strip of land has been occupied for many thousands of years. Earlier even than the megalith men, about 4,000 B.C., there was a race of small, long-legged people living here. Up to the eleventh century Quiberon was

covered in forests, for records show that Duke Alain Canhiart
hunted the deer here. It suffered the usual Viking invasions, then
later attacks by English, Dutch, Germans and Portuguese. The
year 1746 was a particularly black one for Quiberon, when France
and Britain were at war. On the 12th of October an English fleet
disembarked on the peninsula. Most of the inhabitants fled. The
English remained eight days, and did so much damage that when
the Duc de Penthièvre came to inspect it, he released the inhabitants from their taxes for two years.

But apart from the sea battle of 1759, when Admiral Hawke
defeated the French fleet under Conflans, Quiberon is probably
most renowned in history for the ill-fated battle which took place
on one of its beaches, when the Breton Blues, commanded by
Hoche, defeated the émigrés and Chouans in 1795.

A statue to Hoche now stands at the entrance to the pleasant
little park near the front; to one side of it is the Syndicat d'Initiative. This square makes a good starting place for walks and
expeditions.

The best expedition is the one westwards towards the Côte
Sauvage (about 12 km. return), which can be done by car. However, the cliff is so soft and easy to negotiate that walking over it is a
pleasure.

After Port Maria, noted for its sardines, you will eventually find
yourself on a lowish stretch of cliff, where the sea pounds the grey-
brown rocks. But this gradually becomes higher as you proceed.

I found it really beautiful, with its coves, grottoes, tiny inviting
beaches and roaring water, as the sun sank slowly down over the
horizon. Time seemed unimportant as I was lured farther and
farther on. First to the Pointe Beger Goalennec, then the delightful
little ports of Kerné, Guibelleo and Pigeon, until finally I just had
to reach Pointe du Percho. By then the sun had practically sunk
into the sea and it was almost dark.

When I did this walk, I did not know that this coast with its
strange-shaped rocks, and where some of Brittany's oldest prehistoric remains have been excavated, has a very old reputation of
luring people along it: a siren who tries to tempt people to try its

waters. I suppose I might have guessed it was dangerous by the many notices I saw along the coast, warning people against bathing and fishing. Some days later, a Breton friend introduced me to the widow of a man who had fallen in while fishing from this very coast, and whose body had not been found until a week later.

Fortunately, I had enough sense to return to Quiberon via the more prosaic road, rather than risk stumbling back the way I had come in the dark.

The next best walk from Quiberon is the one going in the opposite direction (about eight km. return), turning leftward along the Boulevard Chanard, skirting Quiberon's great beach in the direction of Pointe de Conguel. At its tip is a viewing table from which you can see the islands – Belle Isle, Hoëdic, Houat. If you continue past Fort Neuf and just before Port Haliguen, you will find yourself on the beach where the émigré army met its end. An obelisk marks the spot where they surrendered to General Hoche. The road running behind the beach bears the name Boulevard des Émigrés.

The émigrés had planned to join up with the chouans, and the landings began at Carnac Plage, lasting several days. But the enterprise was badly planned, unlucky and took too long. The Republican army was ready for them and they were driven back to the Quiberon peninsula. When the exiles tried to disembark at Port Haliguen, a heavy swell prevented the British ships from getting near enough to land. About 1,500 men were killed. The wounded were taken to Fort Penthièvre and to the Locmaria church, which was turned into a hospital. Hoche did try to save the lives of those taken prisoner, but the Convention in Paris refused to pardon them.

Boat trips from Quiberon leave from Port Maria or Port Haliguen (weather permitting). You can visit Belle Isle, Hoëdic and Houat, Belle Isle's two small neighbours.

Belle Isle, 84 square kilometres in area and Brittany's biggest and most beautiful island, is a must for anyone staying at Quiberon.

The steamer, quite large and comfortable, does the 15-km. journey in about three-quarters of an hour. You can take your car, but as this is quite expensive anyone making a short day-trip would find it easier and cheaper to hire a car or even a bike on Belle Isle for the day. There are also coach trips round the island during the season.

As you approach Belle Isle's coastline it appears at first as long rocks, emerging out of the sea, dotted with houses and trees; then the Vauban citadel, looming above Le Palais, its main harbour and town, comes into view.

Like Quiberon, Belle Isle has a good climate. Its countryside is varied: sometimes undulating, sometimes wooded, sometimes with desolate stretches of gorse and heather, or cut up into cultivated fields and pastures. There are about 140 'villages' (often hamlets) of whitewashed or grey stone houses, and quite a few hotels and camp sites. Its chief and most attractive feature is its beautiful beaches, stretches of sand fringed with trees and rocks, and many little coves along its rugged and picturesque coast ideal for picknicking and bathing.

Rather surprisingly this apparently peaceful place has had quite a stormy history, chiefly because it was difficult to defend. It was invaded by both Saxons and Normans and then in 1006 it was given by Geoffrey I, Duke of Brittany, to the monks of Redon, who owned it for the next five centuries, when it was under continual attack by enemy fleets. Although Henri II had a fort built there in 1549, it did not prevent the English from landing and occupying the place for three weeks in 1572. Then Charles IX, reckoning that it was too strategic a place to be left in the care of monks, gave it to the Duke of Retz, who improved its fortifications. Later, in 1658, Nicolas Fouquet, Superintendant of Finance for Louis XIV, became its seigneur and built himself a château there, also a fleet, hoping perhaps to make it his own private kingdom. However, his later arrest prevented him from finishing the island's fortifications.

After 1674, when the Dutch had descended on the island, Vauban was charged with improving the fortifications (the citadel and its principal redoubts, Ramonette and Grand Rocher). Even

15   Lace seller at Le Croisic

so, it was blockaded by the English and Dutch from 1696 to 1704. It was blockaded by the English in 1761, when it was finally forced to surrender. However, by the Treaty of Paris of 1763 the English agreed to exchange Belle Isle for the return of Minorca, captured by the French.

In 1765, 78 French Canadian families arrived from Canada (many Bretons had emigrated there in 1632). The eastern province, known as Arcadie, had been surrendered by France and was re-settled by Scots, who re-named it Nova Scotia. These emigrants in reverse were quickly re-integrated into the community, and today Arcadian ancestry is regarded with pride.

Belle Isle suffered during the last war when 10,000 Germans occupied the island, and many of her people were forced to leave. Also, as part of the Lorient pocket zone, Belle Isle was one of the last places in France to be liberated.

In my view, Belle Isle is an ideal place for a family holiday or for those in search of peace, quiet and pleasures such as swimming, sailing, fishing, lazing, walking. But it is definitely not for those who want night life and sophisticated amusements.

Unfortunately, when I visited it, I had chosen the windiest and stormiest day of the year. Each time when my guide and I left the little grey Citroën on the clifftop, I expected to see it picked up by the wind and hurled into the sea.

We started our tour from Le Palais, but I never managed to find out how this town got its name. Surely it could not refer to the grim stark citadel, or even to Fouquet's ruined château beyond. Fouquet's proud family motto – 'How high shall I not climb' – was probably the cause of his very long fall from favour.

We stopped to look at Sauzon (its name means Saxon, after the Saxons who settled there), a very picturesque fishing port, famous for its lobsters and sardines, and situated on the Sauzon river. The Pointe des Poulains ('Colts' Point') was our next stopping place. Near here once stood the actress Sarah Bernhardt's château, over-looking a creek, surrounded by rocks; it was destroyed by the Germans during the war. The fort-like building standing in its place commands a wonderful view of the bay and its

16 Vannes – part of the walls

strange-shaped rocks, such as Les Cochons and the Rocher du Chien, which resembles a crouching dog.

Unfortunately, apart from the wind, it was high tide, so that we were only able to peer down into the famous Grotte d'Apothicairerie on the west side of the island. This got its name because cormorants built their nests along the rocky walls and were supposed to resemble jars on the shelves of a chemist's shop. Alas, these birds have long since flown off, and no longer nest there.

On the next part of our drive towards Port Donnant, we saw the island's two menhirs, affectionately known as Jean and Jeanne. Port Donnant is the prettiest of the island's bays, but rather dangerous for bathing, as are all the coves on the west side, the Côte Sauvage of Belle Isle. The Aiguilles de Port Coton, with its strong waves and line of needle-shaped rocks, stretching out to sea, got its name because the sea there is supposed to build up foam like a mass of cotton wool.

The village of Bangor is the oldest on the island, and its church, dating from 1071, is much plainer than most Breton churches inside. The church at Locmaria is also old, but more attractive, and is the proud possessor of two paintings by Murillo – The Virgin and the Virgin and Child.

Port Andro marks the beginning of the *douce*, the calm sweet side of the island. From here onwards are the bathing beaches, such as the Plage des Grands Sables, Belle Isle's finest and largest stretch of golden sand, backed by low hills.

Quite soon after, we were back at Le Palais. Its main church is worth a visit, as is Vauban's great fort, which has an interesting museum inside. This includes mementoes of Sarah Bernhardt and of the island's occupation during two world wars. In the prison behind, now empty, bleak, ruined and desolate, some important Germans were held after the war, as were some Algerian leaders, such as Ben Bella in 1959.

6. The Loire Atlantique

The Guérande Peninsula

The west side of the Guérande Peninsula is known as the white country because of the heaps of salt collected there from the sea.

As recently as Roman times, the sea stretched between the rocky island of Batz and the Guérande ridge. A change of level turned this gulf into marshes. Batz was linked by sand brought down by currents with the mainland, on the strip of which Le Pouliguen and La Baule now stand.

There is still a gap between Le Penbron, west of Batz, and le Croisic opposite, through which at high tide the sea flows into the old gulf, the Grand and Petit Traits. Mussels, winkles, clams and oysters are gathered from their beds in the mud at low tide. Another part has been laid out in squares whose sides are bounded by low banks of clay soil. These are the Marais Salants (salt pans), where salt crystallizes and is collected and put to dry on little platforms, before being stowed away in sheds.

La Baule, lying eastwards beyond the rocky Pointe Penchâteau, sprawls all around a wide shallow arc of coast. More international than Breton, it comes into the Biarritz/Cannes class, a seaside city of casinos, boulevards, parks and pavilions, and rows of grand hotels. It is expensive, although it claims a wide range of accommodation pricewise.

Its chief attractions are its climate and its five-kilometre sweep of sandy beach. Then there are its sporting facilities – sailing, swimming, tennis, golf, riding (especially horse-racing) and night life – cabarets, night clubs and smart restaurants.

Like Dinard, its north coast counterpart, it is a comparatively recent resort. Up to about a hundred years ago there were only a few villas scattered among its sand dunes and pine groves. It has grown and grown. Today its west side extends and joins up with Le Poulinguen, fishing village and smart yachting harbour, while eastwards lie the scattered groves of La Baule-les-Pins, whose pines help pin down the sand dunes and give shelter from the strong winds.

La Baule, with its excellent communications – road, rail, and air – make it a favourite place for conferences, and a good excursion centre for trips all over Brittany.

Near at hand, you can tour the Guérande peninsula (Drouin Tours do this trip during the season). Drive first to Le Poulinguen, then skirt the Grand Coast, where high cliffs and grottoes make a strong contrast to the low coast round La Baule. Batz, another resort, has an interesting church, St Guénolé (rebuilt in the fifteenth and sixteenth centuries), the tall 180-foot belfry of which can be seen from afar.

Le Croisic, larger, whose picturesque fishing port (sardines and shellfish) is divided by islets, has some attractive seventeenth- and eighteenth-century houses, and a Town Hall built during the reign of Henri iv. Also intricate old alleys lead to its sixteenth-century church, Notre-Dame-de-la-Pitié. Le Croisic is becoming an increasingly popular resort. It faces south, has a good climate and has managed to retain its Breton quaintness in contrast to the more slickly sophisticated La Baule. From its artificial mound, Mont Esprit, which is quite amusing to climb, there is a good view of the salt pens and marshes, and even Belle Isle and the Rhuys peninsula on a fine day.

To get to the salt village of Saillé, you will have to return to Batz (N771 and 774). From Saillé you can drive through the salt marshes to Sissable, or take the D92 to the sardine port of La Turballe, then the D99 to the Pointe Castelli, from which there is a good view of the Rhuys peninsula (right) and the peninsula of Le Croisic (left). The D99 and V9 take you to Piraic, another resort and fishing village. From here, you take the D333 and D99 to Guérande.

The old medieval fortified town of Guérande is another Concarneau, only it stands on a ridge overlooking flat country, lagoons and marshes. It is remarkably well-preserved; its ramparts are complete as are its four fortified gates and eight towers. Guérande is chiefly famous in Breton history as the place where Montfort's victory at Auray, ending the War of Succession, was confirmed. It was here, in the old church of St Aubin, surrounded by a maze of old streets, that the Treaty of Guérande was signed in 1365.

Guérande, immortalized by Balzac in *Beatrice*, is another place best just to wander through. But first walk round its ramparts, then enter the fifteenth-century Porte Michel, the most impressive of the gates. Its towers hold a local museum of Breton furniture and costumes, and also information about the workings of the salt marshes, which in the old days were the city's main source of revenue. The great hall leads back to the ramparts. Should you not have time to visit the town you can drive round the wide, tree-lined promenade which has replaced most of the moat (a bit remains in the north-west), filled in by the Duc d'Aigullon, a Governor of Brittany in the eighteenth century, and which formerly surrounded the town.

After Guérande, before returning to La Baule, you can visit Careil manor house, built in the fourteenth century and restored in the fifteenth and sixteenth centuries; it is renowned for its fireplaces, ceilings, and the collections of Renaissance furniture and seventeenth-century porcelain.

To the east of La Baule lies the Grande Brière, the Black Country, whose swampy land, fed by freshwater streams, produces not salt, but peat. It is a melancholy but picturesque region, of swamps, islets and shining expanses of water, framed by reeds, tamarisks and willows.

The Grande Brière, approximately 20,000 acres, was once a large gulf, rather similar to the Morbihan, but fed by the Vilaine and Loire rivers. Deposits of alluvial soil washing down into it gradually raised its shallow floor, turning it into marshy woodland.

Also the Vilaine and Loire changed their courses. The trees were later to become peat.

During winter, the Grand Brière is flooded, but during spring, when drying, it is covered in flowers. The granite islands, now small hills, have become settlements surrounded by dykes. Of these, the Ile de Fédrun is the most typical and complete of these Briéron 'island' villages. A road within it encircles the low, white-washed cottages. Houses have their own docks and boats (*blains*) for travelling along the canals which now drain the marshes.

Peat is getting rarer. Some people make a living by fishing, hunting water-creatures, raising poultry, or grazing sheep on the patches of pasture land. Others grow reeds for making baskets and chairs, or thatching roofs. Villages all around this area are urged to have a few of their houses thatched in order to preserve their picturesqueness and encourage this industry.

The region is particularly popular with anglers and wild fowlers, who punt through it in the white flat-bottomed boats. There is also a bird sanctuary and nature reserve.

You can circle it by car, starting from St Nazaire. On certain days between June and September, Drouin buses do a tour of it. If you are driving from La Baule you should take the coast road via Pornichet Ste Marguerite and St Marc. You can also go this way by local bus, but check first, as not all of them go via the coast.

Nantes

Nantes, with its cathedral, university, factories, port and aerodrome, sprawling either side of the wide Loire, is a true metropolis, and a great city of France. It has played an important part both in French and Breton history.

Nantes, both Gallic and Roman, was involved in many struggles between Frankish kings and Breton dukes. In 843 it took the brunt of the first Norman attack, before they started on their onslaught of Brittany. But it was below Nantes, nearly a hundred years later, that the young Alain Barbe Torte rallied the people to turn the Normans out of Brittany. Later, as duke, he made Nantes his capital, and rebuilt the city. Nantes, in rivalry with Rennes, was Brittany's capital more than once in the Middle Ages. François II and the Duchess Anne governed as sovereigns from its massive castle on the Loire. Then during the Wars of Religion it was to Nantes that Henri IV came to re-establish and guarantee peace – for a period, that is – by signing the 92 articles of the Edict of Nantes.

Nantes chiefly owed her good fortune to her position on the Loire, which for centuries was a natural highway into the heart of France. Her greatest prosperity was during the sixteenth, seventeenth and eighteenth centuries, and came mainly from the sugar and slave trade (known as the ebony trade). Slaves were sold in the Antilles and cane sugar, bought with the profits, was refined at Nantes, then sent up the Loire. By the end of the eighteenth century Nantes was the first port of France. Fine mansions, built by the shipowners, still line the Quai de la Fosse and the former island of Feydeau.

The abolition of the slave trade, the substitution of French beet for Antilles cane sugar, the silting up of the river, making it difficult for large ships to reach Nantes, brought a decline to Nantes' prosperity and importance. Nantes became an industrial city, turning to metallurgy, iron and steel works, brewing, flour mills and food canning, etc. She is still the heart of a wine-growing region. The vineyards of the flat open country south of the Loire produce Muscadet. You will find plenty of this dry white fruity wine in Nantais cafés and restaurants, as you will all over Brittany.

Today, Nantes with her wide boulevards and parks is a big and busy city with the air of capital. Yet the maze of old streets, little squares, especially around the cathedral, and the stairways and alleys leading down to the port, have retained the Breton quaintness of a provincial centre.

Nantes' medieval and classical architecture are conveniently divided into two districts, which were originally separated by the river Erdre, which flowed into the town from the north (Quai de Versailles), but whose last stretch of water now runs below the wide and curving Cours des 50 Otages. On its east side is the old medieval part, on the west is the newer, classical part.

At the southern end of the Cours des 50 Otages lies the wide Cours Franklin Roosevelt. On a map this area's large shape looks like a boat. The old Rue Kervégan and Avenues Duguay-Trouin and Turenne lie along the old Ile de Feydeau, once an island, but now part of the town. Instead of shining water, they are surrounded by rows of shiny cars in a massive car park, and noisy bus stops.

Brittany has royalist traditions and in the Place Maréchal Foch, once the Place Louis XVI, still stands a column surmounted by this guillotined king's statue.

On the left is the Porte St Pierre, a massive gateway, built at the end of the fifteenth century, and which now holds a museum of pictures illustrating the history of Nantes. Just beside it are some Gallo-Roman remains.

The nearby cathedral of St Peter and St Paul was badly damaged by fire in January 1972. Unfortunately, when I visited it, most of it was barricaded off to the public because the roof was considered unsafe.

Built between 1434 and 1893, it has followed the Breton tradition of slow building. Fortunately this has not damaged the final effect. It has an imposing Gothic façade and an interior of white stone instead of the usual Breton granite. The use of this stone has enabled the builders to build higher and the vaulting, 120 feet high, outstrips even that of Notre Dame in Paris, which is only 110 feet. Fortunately the fire didn't damage the statuary and near the inside door are two of Nantes' heroes, St Rogatian and St Donatian, two young Gallo-Roman soldiers, martyred about A.D. 290. These brothers are represented in the towns' processions by two young men dressed as Roman warriors, walking with their arms round each other's waist.

The most important object in the cathedral, the tomb of François II, a Renaissance objet d'art carved in the early sixteenth century, unfortunately I could not see. Anne of Brittany commissioned it to receive the remains of her father and mother,

Marguerite of Foix, too, and it was originally placed in the church of the Carmelites. During the Revolution the Tribunal ordered its demolition, but the town architect hid various pieces of the tomb in his friends' homes. After the Revolution it was put together again, and in 1817 placed in the cathedral. Alas, the gold cask supposed to contain the heart of Anne of Brittany was found to be empty. This casket is now kept in the Dobrée museum.

The château of the dukes is not far from the cathedral. If you turn left down the Rue Mathelin-Rodier, you will soon arrive at this imposing medieval structure, surrounded by a narrow strip of water, then grass and a wall, and entered by crossing a drawbridge. At one time the south, east and north-east overlooked a branch of the Loire.

The present building was begun by François II in 1466, and his daughter Anne continued the construction. During the Wars of Religion, the Duke of Mercoeur improved on its defences. It was taken over by the military in the eighteenth century, who destroyed some parts of it and added others. Eventually, in 1915, the city of Nantes restored what they could and added two museums.

The castle, like some of the museums in Nantes, is closed on Tuesday, so if you are making a day trip to the town, and you want to see it properly, choose another day. The large courtyard is open every day. You can visit the two museums inside the courtyard, but if you want to see over the castle, you will have to find the *gardien*, as these parts are kept locked. They are worth seeing.

As with so many Breton châteaux, once inside the courtyard the atmosphere changes to that of a palace. Jousting, tournaments and all sorts of performances once took place in its large square. One of the first things you will notice is the rather beautiful well, the delicate iron framework of which is shaped like a ducal crown. If you look down under the netting, put there to prevent children falling in, you will see a crown reflected in the water below.

Behind the well is the Grand Government (the governor's palace), which was rebuilt after a fire in 1684. Next to it, is the Renaissance Gothic *grand logis*, which has five beautifully carved dormer windows, and which was used as a dwelling place for the men-at-arms.

I visited two of the castle's towers, one quite large, with barred windows, where Fouquet (remember Belle Isle) stayed in 1661 before being seized by Louis xiv's men. The other, much larger, its ruins now occupied by pigeons, was a grim and sinister place. It housed many prisoners during the Revolution (priests, Vendéeans, royalists, and other suspects). The interior is now much higher than it was then, because it had once held two floors. Of most interest was the magnificent church carved by prisoners out of the thick castle wall beside the barred window.

At one stage of the Revolution, when Nantes' prisons were overflowing with suspects, the deputy Carrier was sent by the Convention in Paris to purge the town of 'rotten matter'. Carrier solved the problem by arranging to have them all drowned. The prisons were emptied by putting the condemned men in barges, which were conveniently scuttled in the nearby Loire river.

The two museums in the château are worth a visit. One, the museum of local and popular art shows an interesting collection of costumes and especially of the lace caps worn in different parts of Brittany; also there are displays of Breton furniture and interiors of Breton houses. The Salorges museum, which is situated in the lower part of the building opposite, is more technical. Here you can learn about Nantes' slave ships, privateers and navigation on the Loire during her seafaring days of the eighteenth century.

If you are spending the day in Nantes and want to have a picnic lunch, there is a pleasant park (the Jardin des Plantes) not very far from the castle. If you go down the Rue Richebourg and cross the Rue Stanislas Baudry, you will come to it, nearly opposite the station.

It is large, formally laid-out with many rare and exotic plants and trees, numerous pools with pretty little waterfalls, and sheltered arbour walls. There is a statue of Jules Verne, who was born in Nantes, at one end of the garden.

Apart from the château and castle, there is not a lot to see in Nantes, and heavy traffic makes walking through the old town hazardous. Still it is a pleasant city, if you can manage to forget the cars. The following route makes a fairly representative walk.

Start outside the cathedral in the Place St Pierre, continue down the Rue de Verdun into the Rue de la Marne and the Place de Change (you will find the Syndicat d'Initiative here). Near by is the old church of St Croix. Then continue and cross over the wide Cours des 50 Otages and up the Rue d'Orléans to the Place Royale, a very pleasant square with a large fountain in the centre (1865), representing the Loire and its tributaries. To one side of the square is the church of St Nicholas, which you might care to visit. The Place Royale leads into the Rue Crébillon, narrow, steep, and generally crowded for it has some good shops. The Place Graslin, which it leads into is quite a fine square. The Grand Théâtre is situated there.

From here you can either continue along the Rue Voltaire to the Dobrée and Archaeological museum, named after a Nantais collector of that name (manuscripts, ceramics, enamels, ecclesiastical jewellery, paintings, furniture, weapons and a historical section, etc.) in the Place Jean V, and the museum of Natural History in the Place de la Monnaie, or you can walk from the Place Graslin into the Cours Cambronne, a wide tree-shaded walk, very French, and lined with trim eighteenth-century houses, all alike. In its centre stands the aggressive figure of the Nantais general, after whom it is named, and who is chiefly remembered for his answer, which included *'merde'* (very rude word in French) when called upon to surrender to the English at Waterloo. What happened next, I did not discover, but he survived until 1842.

Turn right from here into the Rue de Bréa and along the Place Sanitaire, down the Rue Mazagraw into the Place St Jean l'Herminer and the Quai de la Fosse. You should now find yourself beside the port. If you find harbours and shipyards interesting, you might enjoy turning right in the direction of the Belvédère Ste Anne. But it is rather a smelly, dirty and noisy walk.

You will see the road leading up to the Belvédère Ste Anne after about 15 minutes of walking. At the top is a garden and table of orientation with a good view of the river and the busy harbour below. The table will tell you which of the various steeples and towers you can see is which, but the tangle of cranes and funnels provides a fairly formidable curtain. You can see the cathedral, but not the château. To the right of centre is the Cité Radieuse, built by Le Corbusier, and an experiment in modern living. The 300 flats have their own infant school, cinema and swimming pool.

Further along to the right, but impossible to see from this position, is Chantenay, where in June 1793, the notorious drownings in the Loire took place.

Part 2
Normandy

7. History and Introduction

Normandy divides into two geographical sections; higher in the east and lower in the west. Higher Normandy, with its rich open chalklands and orchards, lies chiefly to the north of the Seine and is made up of the two departments, Seine Maritime and Eure. Lower Normandy, less fertile and merging with Brittany, is made up of Orne, Calvados and the Manche.

There are probably few other places in the world where an English person would feel more at home than Normandy. The fields and hedgerows, sleepy farms and villages, ruined castles, cathedrals, churches and old manor houses, even the damp mild climate, would remind him of southern England, especially Devonshire. Normandy has played an important part in our island's history and much in our culture originated in this lush green maritime province of northern France.

Normandy owes its name to the Norsemen who settled there in the ninth century. They held the mouth of the Seine and steered their dragon-prowed boats up its wide loops as far as Paris, which they raided four times. Finally in 911 the French king wisely made a treaty at Clair-sur-Epte with their leader, Rollo. This gave them the right to settle over a large area of the province we know now as Normandy. In return, the Vikings were supposed to accept Christianity and perform military service for the Carolingian kings.

Although Rollo was baptized in 912 he is said to have died a pagan, as were most of his Norsemen. However, his son, William

Longsword (William I), was converted and extended Norman rule, wresting territory from the Bretons in the west.

It took the Norman dukes about 150 years to consolidate their power and position. They had to withstand the attempts of the French kings to bring their duchy more under their own control, establish their rule over the Frankish population already living in the duchy and over their own Norse nobles, as well as keep out other dukes from the province.

The Normans retained many of the Viking characteristics. Ruthless and reckless, courageous and crafty, a mere handful of them could vanquish an enemy of far larger numbers.

They were also quick to imitate and adapt. They didn't invent castle building, but soon became masters of it, while they took to horse-riding as if to the manner born. They proved efficient and progressive rulers, adapting and improving on the institutions they found in newly-conquered territories. Under their rule Sicily became one of the most prosperous states in the Mediterranean.

These former pagan pirates became the advocates of the civilization they had previously attacked, becoming strong exponents of feudalism and champions of the Church. The patronage of their dukes enabled the religious centres of Benedictine learning to flourish. Pilgrimages to Rome and the Holy Land, although inspired more by love of conquest and adventure than religious devotion, were very popular with the Normans.

Also, the growth of the Norman population soon outstripped its territory. As many Norman nobles and younger sons had few prospects of inheritance at home, they were obliged to seek their fortunes farther afield.

Fortunately, the Normans had integrated well with the Frankish population. Their dukes, who had unusual political ability made their province one of the best organized feudal states in Europe. Although still technically a fief of the French king, it was independent and strong enough in 1066 to launch a successful attack against England.

William II of Normandy (William I of England) did have some

17 Rouen cathedral from the east

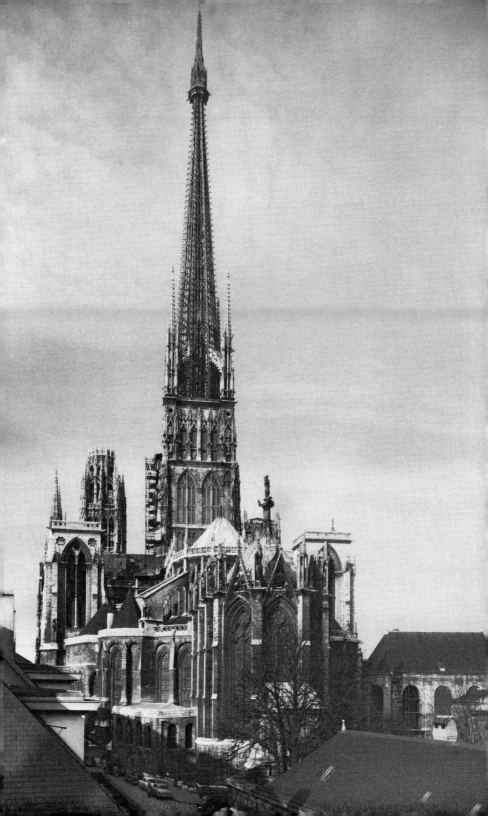

18 *Coutances Cathedral, Manche*   19 *Old still and pots of herbs at the Bénédictine distillery of the monastery at Fécamp*

justification for his claim to the English throne. When he learned that Harold had been made king, he sent emissaries to remind Harold of his former promise – that he should renounce the throne in favour of William. Harold ignored this and William called in the Pope to support his claim. The Pope did so, and excommunicated Harold. William then convened a meeting of his barons at Lillebonne and won their support; he next persuaded Harald Hardrade of Norway to attack Harold in the north.

Harold, after destroying the Viking army at Stamford Bridge, hurried south to do battle with William on 14 October near Hastings. By nightfall he and his earls lay dead, and his army was defeated. William's coronation took place in Westminster Abbey on Christmas Day. He celebrated Easter in Normandy. In 15 months he had conceived an expedition, launched it, and captured a kingdom and a crown.

However, England was a pretty sizeable lump to digest quickly, and he still had to keep his own province in order. While he was abroad William's cousin and consort, Mathilda of Flanders, had ruled Normandy with the help of their eldest son, Robert, who, aided by the French king, rebelled against his father. William died in 1087 during an expedition against the French king.

The union of Normandy and England was broken. Robert became duke as Robert II, while England passed to his brother, who became its king as William II. The two brothers were not long at peace. Robert was supported by the French king and William II was helped by his brother, Henry. On William II's death, Robert's designs on England were frustrated by Henry, who became its next king as Henry I.

Despite negotiations, the quarrels continued. In 1106 Henry, after defeating Robert at the battle of Tinchebray, became Duke of Normandy himself.

The then French king, Louis VI, took up the cause of Robert's son, but Henry I had his own son recognized as the heir of Normandy. In 1119 Louis VI and Robert's son were decisively defeated at Bremule in the Vexin. However, Henry's son was drowned at sea and Robert's son died in 1128; when Henry himself died in 1135 it was the end of the male line of the house of Rollo.

The Norman succession was in dispute until 1144, when Geoffrey Plantagnet, Count of Anjou and second husband of Henry I's daughter, Mathilda, won Normandy from the rival house of Blois. He and Mathilda gave the duchy to their son, Henry, in 1150. Henry inherited Anjou and Maine from his father in 1151, then acquired Aquitaine by his marriage with Eleanor in 1152. He became king of England as Henry II in 1154.

This union of England and Normandy had considerable effect on both their histories. Norman rulers had remained true to the Conqueror's promise in Westminster Abbey – the structure of English government remained Anglo-Saxon, but was under efficient Norman direction and innovation. England had a centralized government and well organized church and, most important, had been made safe from invasion. Norman French, at first the language of the ruling class and the legal language until 1400, was gradually incorporated into English, greatly enriching it.

Normandy was a model feudal state. Because the king could not be in both places at once, he had to delegate and institutionalize many of his functions, thus enabling political institutions to develop in both countries.

Then the Normans were great builders. Towns, abbeys, cathedrals, churches and castles were erected. The material was near at hand. Around Rouen was the soft stone found in the chalky cliffs bordering the river. Around Caen in the Calvados was the oolithic limestone known as Caen stone. Farther west were sandstone and granite similar to those found in Brittany. The Benedictines, protected by the dukes, had a long tradition of architecture, inherited from the Romans, but which they improved on. The Norman style, an imitation of Romanesque, was of bolder proportions, with pure lines and sober, geometric-type ornamentation.

However, Henry II's marriage with Eleanor was to cause deep trouble between France, Normandy and England. The French king had no option but to try and weaken such a powerful vassal. Although it was agreed that the French king's infant daughter should marry Henry's eldest son, taking with her as dowry the Vexin Normand and Gisors, warfare between the kings continued. The next French king, Philippe II (Philippe Auguste) demanded the surrender of Vexin in 1187 on the grounds that Henry's son had died in 1183 and that the newly projected marriage of the latter's brother, Richard, to Alice, another French princess, had not taken place.

Philippe also supported Richard, then a close friend, against his father in the rebellion which hastened Henry's death. However, Philippe and Richard did not remain friends long. In spite of a Treaty made in Sicily in 1191 on the way to a crusade, Philippe tried to annexe the Vexin and the town of Gisors with the aid of Richard's brother, John, while the Lionheart languished in a prison in Germany.

On release Richard won a great victory over Philippe at Fréteval, near Vendôme, in 1194. To protect the Vexin and bar the French king's way into France along the Seine, he built Château Gaillard, a massive fortress overlooking the river, in 1196. After another victory at Courcelles in 1199, Philippe only had the border town of Gisors left in Normandy.

Philippe didn't have to wait long. After Richard's death his brother John inherited the Norman and English crowns. But Philippe, like the Bretons and many Normans, supported the claims of Arthur, John's nephew. John's later alleged murder of Arthur gave him the excuse to invade Normandy in 1202. Château Gaillard fell after a long siege and Rouen capitulated in 1204. By then all Normandy belonged to the King of France, a fact finally acknowledged by the English crown when Henry III (England) and Louis IX (France) signed the Treaty of Paris in 1259.

The French king's administration found much to learn and admire about good government in Normandy. Communes with their own charters were already established. Arbitrary levying of taxes and services was much resented. The French kings were obliged to abide by the *Charte aux Normands* (1314–15), guaranteeing the duchy's rights and privileges.

By the Treaty of Paris Henry had retained the Duchy of Guienne, for which he had to do homage to the French king, and was allowed certain territory which protected its borders. Later kings tried to evade this agreement. French officials often interfered in Guienne. There were skirmishes at sea, kings who refused to do proper homage, destruction of forts, retaliations.

The spark that was to set off the fire was the question of the succession to the French throne. When Charles iv died in 1328 leaving no male heir, the principal claimants were Edward iii (through his mother) and Philippe vi (then Count of Valois), son of Philippe iv's brother, Charles.

An Assembly of Magnates decided in favour of Philippe. Edward at first protested, but later withdrew his claim. He did simple homage for Guienne in 1329, but Philippe demanded liege honour and refused to restore lands Edward was claiming. The cold war began in earnest. Edward intrigued in the Low Countries against Philippe, Philippe intrigued in Scotland against Edward.

The Hundred Years' War could be said to have started when Philippe confiscated Guienne in 1337, and Edward declared that France should be his.

Hostilities began at sea between privateers. Edward iii went to Antwerp, where he got the support of the Low Countries and defeated the French fleet at Sluis in 1340. Operations next shifted to Brittany where Edward supported John of Montfort against Charles de Blois. He also fomented rebellion in the west of France.

Edward landed in the Cotentin in 1346 and took Caen, crossed the Seine at Poissy, and set out for Picardy. Philippe caught up with him at Crécy where the French army was defeated. It seemed as if everything was going for Edward. The Scots were defeated at Neville Cross while Charles de Blois had defeats in Brittany. However, the Black Death, which favoured neither side, brought the war to a temporary standstill.

Hostilities broke out again in 1355 when the Black Prince

landed at Bordeaux, ravaged the countryside, defeated the French king, Jean II, at Poitiers, and took him prisoner. The period that followed was one of ravaging and pillaging and of great misery for France.

By the Treaty of Brétigny in 1360 France ceded the whole of Aquitaine, also Calais and Guienne, to the English but not Normandy. Charles V (who had been made Duke of Normandy in 1355 by Jean II) began his reign as king of France by sending Du Guesclin to drive the English out of Normandy. This time the English armies and fleet were defeated.

The following years were relatively peaceful. Edward III and the Black Prince died. Richard II and the next French king, Charles VI, were only boys when they came to their thrones and were later too busy with their own countries to take up the squabble.

However, this was changed when Henry IV succeeded Richard, and Louis, brother of a now partly insane Charles VI, tried to make trouble for Henry by helping the Welsh Owen Glendower. Henry IV started on the reconquest of Aquitaine, lost by Richard II. This was continued by Henry V, who landed at the Chef du Caux in 1413. He took Harfleur in 1415, then routed the French army at Agincourt.

In 1417 Henry began the methodical subjugation of Normandy, town by town, district by district. Caen, Alençon, Evreux, opened their gates to him. Henry seized Rouen, the Pays de Caux and Vexin. His next step was to try and disinherit the French Dauphin and make his own house rulers of France.

By the Treaty of Troyes in 1420 Henry was to marry Cathérine, one of Charles VI's daughters. The resulting child would rule both countries. It would be a dual monarchy with each kingdom retaining its own institutions. Again nature took a hand. Henry V died in 1422, as did Charles VI. The son of Henry V and Cathérine was still a mere child.

Then the Dauphin, son of Charles VI, proclaimed himself king of France as Charles VII. The Duke of Bedford, chosen to govern the French territories in the name of the infant Henry, invaded the Loire Valley and in 1428 laid siege to Orleans, which he intended to use as a base against further attacks on Charles's stronghold in the south.

This was where the legendary Joan of Arc came upon the scene. She persuaded Charles VII's captain to send her to Charles's court at Chinon. After she had gained the king's confidence she went with a small force to relieve Orléans. Whether the English would have gone anyway is a matter of conjecture, as their force was only a small one, but their departure probably had a psychological effect on French morale. In 1429 the English were defeated at Patay and Charles VII was crowned at Rheims.

Joan took part in several expeditions. In 1430 she went to Compiégne to help strengthen the defence against the Burgundian ruler, Philip the Good, who was in alliance with the Duke of Bedford. During a sortie she was captured by the Burgundians, who sold her to the English. She was later tried at Rouen, adjudged a heretic, and supposedly burned in the market place on 30 May 1431.

From now onwards English fortunes in Normandy faltered. Philip the Good signed a treaty with the French king, Charles VII, ending the war between France and Burgundy. The very capable Duke of Bedford died in 1435.

Although the English had established a Council of Normandy emphasizing the duchy's separateness from France, and although they had founded a university at Caen, there had always been a certain amount of resistance to their régime. After all, Normandy was attached to France, the people now spoke the same language. There were risings in the Pays de Caux and the Val de Vire.

Also by now France and England were exhausted and wanted to negotiate. By a truce England retained Maine, Bordelaise, the Pas de Calais and most of Normandy. But because they were slow in honouring their agreement the French took several towns from them and started on the reconquest of Normandy. Sir Thomas Kyriel landed in Cherbourg supposedly to reinforce the Duke of Somerset at Caen. Instead he besieged Valognes, giving the French time to close in on him, and forcing him to give battle at Formigny. His defeat there marked the end of British rule in Normandy.

Louis XI, now king, gave the duchy to his brother, Charles, in 1465, but soon took it back. In 1486 he persuaded the French Estates General at Tours to declare Normandy inalienable from the French crown. After this Normandy was governed as a province, although the *Charte aux Normands* was theoretically maintained.

Little was created architecturally during the Hundred Years' War. After it, the style known as Flamboyant Gothic was particularly popular in Rouen and Upper Normandy. Rich merchants built tall houses, partly timbered, partly of stone, with wide eaves and decorated corbels and beams. Good examples of these can still be seen at Rouen, Bayeaux and Honfleur.

Georges d'Amboise, Archbishop of Rouen, who introduced the Italian Renaissance into French building, had much influence on Norman architecture. Examples of this luxurious, exuberant, sophisticated style are to be seen at his castle, Gallion, another is the west door of Rouen cathedral.

The Renaissance style reached its greatest heights in domestic architecture. Older buildings, such as the Château d'O and Fontaine-Henri, were ornamented and added to; parks and gardens replaced fortifications. Gothic survived chiefly in the small manor houses – Renaissance mansions, where a plain outer façade often hid a richly designed inner courtyard, were usually built in towns.

As many Normans were Huguenots, the province suffered badly during the Wars of Religion. There was particular bitter fighting between 1561 and 1563, and from 1574 to 1576. Caen, with its new university, was a particular hotbed of Protestantism, as were the seaports, which had many contacts with England and Holland.

Protestant Henri IV vanquished 30,000 men of the Catholic League in 1589 at Arques and the Leaguers of Mayenne in 1590 at Ivry-la-Bataille. The Edict of Nantes, which he signed in 1598, brought religious peace – for a time anyway – to the province and to France.

Later, in 1685, the Revocation of the Edict of Nantes by

Louis xiv led to a massive emigration of Huguenots from Normandy. As many of them were well-to-do, hard-working and highly skilled, it severely damaged the Norman economy. However, the province was too fertile and its inhabitants too industrious for it to suffer long. By the eighteenth century it had recovered its prosperity.

The seventeenth century had been a time of exploration and expansion overseas: both Quebec and New Orleans were founded by Normans.

Another architectural rebirth had taken place after the Wars of Religion, when many beautiful châteaux were built. A strong Catholic reaction during the first half of the seventeenth century had led to the Jesuits building many colleges and chapels, but in the formal classical style. However, the grand century of building in Normandy was the eighteenth, especially in the towns, where magnificent episcopal palaces and town halls were erected.

As in other parts of France, revolutionary ideas fomented in Normandy. Many Normans served in the new republic. But although they favoured reforms they were naturally hard-headed and conservative with a dislike of excess. By 1793 Caen was the centre for the Girondists, the party of moderation, who opposed the extremists, the Montagnards, based in Paris. During the trial of Louis xvi, 30,000 citizens of Rouen demonstrated in favour of appeal. However, the King's execution and the French army's reverses in the Netherlands led to the ruin of the Girondist party. On 2 June 1793 the Convention in Paris, surrounded by 80,000 armed insurgents, capitulated and ordered the arrest of 29 Girondin deputies. Most of them managed to escape, and tried to raise Normandy, Brittany, Franche Comté, and the south and south-west of France against the government.

Charlotte Corday (1768–93) was living with her aunt in Caen when these refugees arrived, calling for separation from the government and urging military action against the capital. The young Charlotte, deeply moved by events, set off for Paris. She managed to get an interview with the notorious Jean-Paul Marat in his bath, drew the knife from under her dress, and stabbed him through the heart. On the same day insurgent Normans marching on Paris were defeated at Pacy-sur-Eure. Charlotte was sentenced to death by the revolutionary tribunal and executed on 17 July, while in October of that year 31 Girondins were executed.

In November, the army of the Vendée (a coastal department in west France), composed mostly of Catholics and Royalists marched north to raise the Cotentin, but were unsuccessful in capturing the town of Granville. Although they retreated and were finally defeated at Savenoy, opposition to Paris and its interference still remained strong. Warfare continued in the Cotentin and the wooded Bocage, where it was easy to hide. It took the form of ambushes, surprise attacks and raids on government forces and officials, under the direction of Count Louis de Frotté from Alençon. He was eventually caught and shot with five of his companions at Verneuil in 1800.

The nineteenth century was an era of prosperity and peaceful expansion for Normandy. A railway was built between Paris and Rouen in 1843. The Duchess of Berry started a vogue for sea-bathing at Dieppe. The Côte Fleurie became a popular playground for the wealthy of many countries. Good light, wide skies, broad rivers, estuaries and attractive seascapes attracted many artists, especially impressionists, to work on the Normandy coast. Two of France's best-known nineteenth-century writers, Guy de Maupassant and Gustave Flaubert, were both Normans and worked in Normandy.

Normandy's greatest disaster came in the mid-twentieth century, in World War Two, when beaches along the Côte Nacre and the nearby Cotentin peninsula served as a bridgehead for the allied invasion of Europe. More than 200,000 buildings were demolished. Towns, villages, farms and railways had all to be painstakingly rebuilt, a massive task.

Nevertheless it is still a prosperous province, renowned chiefly for its agriculture, especially wheat and dairy produce. It is the home of many famous cheeses; its butter is reckoned to be the best in the world, as is its sparkling apple cider. Livestock rearing, especially horse-breeding, predominates in Lower Normandy.

There are also some important industries – cars, ships, steel, to mention a few; and some small local ones, such as pottery, woodwork, ironwork, copperware and basketry.

Because of its geographical position Normandy acts as a natural corridor from its ports, Cherbourg, Le Havre and Dieppe, to Paris and other parts of France. Many Britishers pass through it on their way south. Although many of the fine old Norman cities and towns suffered so badly in the war, a number of the cathedrals and churches were spared, and the rest have been restored with great care. There is still much old and interesting to see.

Most of this pleasant province is worth exploring, either by car, bus, or – even more leisurely – by bicycle. Less cut off from France, its people are more mixed racially than the Bretons. Even so, you will still see many tall, blue-eyed, fair-skinned people, the unmistakable descendants of those long-ago Vikings.

8. Seine Maritime

Dieppe and its Surroundings

Dieppe, one of France's busiest and most attractive ports, is the best place to start in Normandy.

One's first glimpse of its spires, tall houses and hotels, set between high cliffs, should be more exciting than it is. Unfortunately, the only frontal position from which you can see the town emerging over the horizon is from Sealink's Smoking Lounge, through a glass window, past a barrier of rope coils and all the varied paraphernalia of a large ferry boat.

However, to compensate for this the port is a long one. The ship seems to sail right into the town, cutting deep into Normandy, past gardens, beaches and picturesque old streets and houses.

Dieppe, France's oldest resort, is always regarded as an eighteenth-century town. It suffered two disasters during the seventeenth century : the first was a plague, which broke out in 1668 and in which 10,000 people died, the second was when the English and Dutch fleets bombarded the town in 1694, reducing all the wooden houses in the centre to rubble. Only those buildings made of stone survived; most had to be rebuilt. The eighteenth century was a fortunate period for architecture and the brick houses, built by the architect M. de Vertbroun, were of a sombre elegance, enhanced by the Louis XIV and Louis XV wrought-iron balconies, made by the renowned ironworkers of Arques and Dieppe.

Dieppe became famous as a sea-bathing place after the Restoration, when it was made fashionable by the Duchess of Berry. Later, unattractive hotels and boarding-houses mushroomed up alongside its dunes, shingle beach and sea. Even so, there was enough of the picturesque around the town to attract many artists, especially English ones such as Sickert, Bonington, Beardsley and Turner, to paint there.

Fortunately for Dieppe its war damage was chiefly confined to the unattractive hotels and boarding-houses along the front, while the picturesque part lost only a few buildings. A new front has been laid out, a new casino built, as have many new flats and hotels, also a new Town Hall. All this, plus its port, which although not a great one manages to combine many activities – passengers, fish and fruit – makes it a lively place to visit, and particularly popular with English day-trippers. Incidentally, the best day on which to visit Dieppe is a Saturday, preferably in the morning, when the big market is held.

Dieppe's cafés and restaurants are probably its greatest draw, especially to eat the seafood: sole, mackerel, herring, fish soup and particularly coquilles St Jacques. It is reckoned that two out of every five shellfish eaten in France will have been caught by Dieppe fishermen. The most reasonably-priced restaurants, though perhaps a little shabby to look at, are those along the Quai Henri iv to the right of the Gare Maritime. At Chez Lola you can get a good meal for just under a pound.

Apart from day-trippers, most English travellers to France will have passed through Dieppe at one time or another. It is usually regarded as a milestone, marking the way into or out of France. Nevertheless, it is worth looking round.

The best old thing to see is the sixteenth to nineteenth century collection of ivory in the castle, which was occupied by the Germans during the war and stands atop a hill overlooking both town and front. (The castle was built between 1435 and 1635, and replaces an earlier wooden one burned down during a battle in 1195; it survived the bombardment of 1694.) Many craftsmen came to Dieppe to carve the ivory tusks imported from Africa and the Orient. By the seventeenth century there were 350 of them living in the town. Today, there is only one !

The best old church to see is St Jacq, which has been considerably restored and combines a mixture of centuries. Its nave is thirteenth century, its central doorway fourteenth, its façade tower fifteenth, its east end and their chapels sixteenth, the dome above the transept, eighteenth. The whole could be called a mixture of Flamboyant Gothic and Renaissance, the interior being much plainer than the exterior.

For interest note the little window through which the priest could look down on the people below; it is above the choir, the woodwork of which is so fine that it resembles lace. Also note the frieze above the sacristy door, which shows a line of Brazilian Indians and commemorates the explorers of Dieppe. It was originally in Jean Ango's palace, which was destroyed in the bombardment of 1694.

Jean Ango was a master shipbuilder who during the sixteenth century constructed a fleet of privateers in answer to the Portuguese, who treated as pirates any ships found off West Africa other than their own. Jean Ango's fleet captured 300 Portuguese ships and forced the Portuguese king to change his policy. When Jean retired from the sea in 1530 he built himself a splendid palace in Dieppe, but alas, of wood. However, his country residence, the Manoir d'Ango, can still be visited.

Dieppe's chief tourist attraction is its front, one and a half kilometres of beach, which lies between sea and town. It is difficult to believe that this stretch of shingle and grassy promenade was one of the landing points between Berneval and Ste Marguerite when Operation Jubilee was launched on 19 August 1942. The objective, the capture of Dieppe, was not achieved, but it was the dress rehearsal for the allied invasion of Europe two years later. Over 5,000 men were killed or taken prisoner. Of that number about 1,000 Canadians died in this stretch of water.

Beside the bathing beach are now situated the children's playground, a miniature golf course, a roller-skating track, tennis courts and swimming pool, not forgetting the casino.

Altogether Dieppe has had five casinos, their dates of construction being 1832, 1857, 1887 (very Eastern this one with a dome and minarets), 1928 (this was dynamited by the Germans in order to improve their defences in 1942) and 1961. This last was designed by the architect Tougard, to fit in with the general layout of the front. Open all the year round, it contains a cinema, theatre, dance hall, restaurant and club as well as the rooms where boule, roulette, baccarat and blackjack are played.

Dieppe is within easy reach by car of the forests of Eu and Eawy. Eawy forest, 16,000 acres, is one of the most beautiful stretches of beech woodland in Normandy. Nearer still to Dieppe is the forest of Arques. It was here, incidentally, that the V2s were launched at England in World War Two. The small industrial town of Arques-la-Bataille played an important part in Normandy's history as being the place where Henri iv with only 7,000 men defeated the 30,000-strong army of the Catholic League.

Tréport, about 30 km. north of Dieppe, is Normandy's last town on this coast. It is set on the south side of the river Bresle, which for most of its course marks the boundary between Normandy and Picardy.

Tréport, a small fishing port and popular family resort, is still picturesque with its long shingle beach backed by tall cliffs, as is its twin, Mers-le-Bain, on the opposite bank of the Bresle and in Picardy.

Chair lifts at Tréport transport people to the top of the cliff behind the town. From the terraces there are fine views of the coast and harbour below. Both Tréport and Mers are good places to stay at, as they have all amenities, plus very nice air. The chief snag is they tend to get very crowded during the season as they are within too easy reach of Paris.

Tréport has a long history and was a maritime port even in Roman times. Up to the twelfth century it even disputed supremacy with Dieppe. Then it became silted up owing to a diversion made to the course of the river Bresle. It was burned down several times by the English during the Hundred Years' War and again in 1545. The town and port came into its own again during the time of Louis Philippe and even Queen Victoria twice honoured it with her presence. Tréport had a bad time during the

Second World War, when it suffered severe bombardment and many people were killed. It was awarded the Croix de Guerre with a star of bronze for the courage shown by its inhabitants.

The Alabaster Coast

Southwards from Dieppe lies the Pays de Caux, a rolling chalk country of prosperous farmland, majestic and green, and stretches of beech woods. Particularly attractive are the large, half-timbered Tudor-looking farmhouses with their old stone barns. You will probably notice many tethered cattle in the fields, a custom peculiar to this part of the province.

The tall white cliffs of the Alabaster Coast, continually eroded by sea and weather and cut by deep narrow leafy valleys, make up the most impressive part of Normandy's coastline. That there are few sandy beaches along here may have been to its advantage, preventing over-development and excessive commercialization. The resorts along here are much smaller than those farther south.

Pourville, very pleasantly situated near jagged cliffs and severely damaged during the Dieppe raid, has now been rebuilt. Both Varengeville and Ste Marguerite are a little distance from the sea, but as if in compensation, they are set in very pretty wooded surroundings in a typical Norman countryside of old timbered farmhouses, thatched cottages and small manor houses. Not far away is the splendid, carefully restored Ango manor, mentioned earlier. Ste Marguerite has a particularly attractive twelfth to thirteenth-century church with a beautiful interior. At Quiberville, about 5 km. away, is a sandy beach.

Veules-les-Roses, situated in a sheltered valley with cliffs either side, manages to combine casualness with smartness. Its beach, shingle at high tide, becomes a broad stretch of sand at low. This village resort caters particularly for children. St Valéry, once a fishing and coastal trading port, has only fairly recently become a seaside resort. Its centre was razed in 1940 by units of the British 10th Army, driven back to the sea by the Germans after the collapse of the Somme front. Two memorials to this event stand on the Aval and Amont cliffs. Veulettes, spread over a wide green valley between cliffs, is an attractive if quiet resort.

The most picturesque part of this coast lies between Senneville and Fécamp. Fécamp, due to its famous fishing port – France's fourth largest and the most important for cod – and Holy Trinity church, is a well-known town.

Its quays, old houses and narrow streets lying between long and narrow cliff-like hills have a sort of charm, but it is too commercial and industrialized a place to spend a holiday there. Its church, larger than many a cathedral, is worth a visit, as is the Benedictine distillery and museum. Bénédictine is supposed to have originated at Fécamp : in 1510 a monk called Vincelli had the idea of distilling liquor from the aromatic plants which he found growing on the nearby cliffs.

The church of the Trinity owes its size to the fact that it was the abbey church of a Benedictine foundation. There had been a monastery here since the seventh century. Its main task was to provide shelter for the holy relic of some of Christ's holy blood, lost on the cross. According to tradition, this had been miraculously found in a hollowed-out fig tree beside a spring, which has now been made into a fountain.

Richard I built the church, but it was rebuilt in the twelfth and thirteenth centuries after being struck by lightning, then reconstructed several times between the fifteenth and eighteenth centuries. The monastery, some of which is now restored and forms part of the Town Hall and museum, became very important when Richard II persuaded monks of the reformed Cluniac Order to take up residence there. For a time it was the leading place of pilgrimage in Normandy. Pilgrims still come even now on the Tuesday and Thursday following Trinity Sunday to worship the Holy Blood relic.

Etretat, about 20 km. farther along the coast, is my favourite of the Alabaster Coast resorts. It was particularly popular with artists and writers, such as Maupassant, in the last century, and is an intriguing mixture of character and smartness.

20   *The college chapel at Eu, Seine Maritime*

Its beach, unfortunately shingle, lies between two rocky cliffs. From the right-hand side one, the Amont, surmounted by a small chapel, the first and unsuccessful attempt to fly the Atlantic was made. On the left is the Aval, whose rocky arch, the Port Aval, has been compared most aptly to an elephant plunging his trunk into the water. The sea here is very rough.

An attractive and elegant town lies behind the beach. Note the old wooden market place, housing fruit, vegetable and antique shops and an art gallery, topped by a tower with a splendid old granny clock, wrong of course! It also did good service as a hospital for British and American soldiers in the First World War.

Le Havre

The first time I visited Le Havre, I travelled by bus, and arrived, so to speak by its back door. It was a come down. First, in the distance, loomed the tall skyscrapers, then suddenly, the bus came to a halt in what seemed to be the middle of nowhere in particular, surrounded by half-constructed buildings, untidy land and ugly hoardings. I was quite amazed when I was told that we were actually there. *'Centre ville?'* I asked, non-believing. *'Centre ville. Ici.'* A man beckoned me to follow him through the dilapidated bus station and out the other side. And there it was! Which goes to show that one should never judge by first impressions.

The best way to approach Le Havre is to come down into it from the coast. Then it does really look like what it is, a splendid, brand-new, well-laid-out city. The area that I had first seen was still in the process of becoming part of this.

Le Havre owes its existence to the French king, François I, who ordered its construction in 1517 to replace the older ports of Harfleur and Honfleur. It was first named after him, being known as Francispolis, and was given his coat of arms, a salamander on a red field. This last the town still retains, but the name was soon changed to Le Havre ('the harbour') de Grâce (the name of this piece of the coast).

21 *The Abbey of Jumièges, near Rouen*

The town prospered. By the end of the eighteenth century it had a population of 20,000 people. Trade with the West Indies, and especially with America during the War of Independence against England, brought considerable wealth to the town. It grew richer still in the nineteenth and twentieth centuries. During the First World War its harbour was one of the main supply bases for the Allied armies. During the Second World War it was less fortunate. Le Havre had the dubious honour of being the most badly damaged port on the continent, losing something like 10,000 buildings. The battle for Normandy by-passed it – even Paris was liberated before Le Havre. Even so, although the Germans had blown up all the harbour installations before it was finally taken, the Americans managed to use it as a base. But it took two years to clear away all the town's rubble.

The building of the new town was entrusted to Le Perret, that father of modern architecture. The result, considered a model of all a town should be, includes the residential area of Ste Addresse, the old port of Harfleur, and combines France's most important transatlantic harbour with a busy industrial centre.

Le Havre, like so many of Normandy's newly-constructed cities, which seem to be built more for traffic than the careless saunterer, is best explored by car. I have two criticisms to make about its streets. One, from the point of view of the pedestrian, is that the yellow-striped zebras across wide roads without traffic lights make crossing very hazardous, especially as French drivers aren't noted for their patience. The other, from the point of view of the motorist, is that street names, often in the same beige colour as the buildings, are difficult to read. A driver might well need a telescope.

The best place to start on a tour of the town is from the Town Hall square. The Town Hall, a plain, no-nonsense building with a tall clock tower, overlooks a formal symmetrical garden, surrounded by a wall of plane trees, quite pleasant but rather noisy to sit in.

From here you drive down the Rue de Paris, smartish shops either side, into the Place Général de Gaulle with its large war memorial in the centre, and a dock for boats on one side, spanned by a modern bridge, itself resembling some sort of super-yacht.

The square seems to be surrounded by boxes, all beige and similar, but then the whole of Le Havre is like a city of big horizontal or vertical boxes.

It is also a city by the sea. If you drive back to the Town Hall, then leftwards and westwards down Boulevard Foch, most grand with grass verges and park to one side, you will arrive at the sea front. The beach is pebbly, but sandy further out and popular for bathing, as all the rows of white bathing huts testify.

Then turn left into the Boulevard François 1 towards the ultra-modern St Joseph's Church, the steeple of which resembles a well-sharpened pencil pointing to the sky. This is regarded as one of Auguste Perret's greatest achievements. When you enter, the interior seems to be lit by a milliard coloured lights, streaming through the glass panes. In all there are 12,768 pieces of glass, in 50 different shades of colour, but with gold predominating, and in many different shapes, sizes and patterns. Each colour has a meaning, as does its position; the light within the church varies according to the time of day. The church furniture has been specially arranged to induce a community spirit. The altar is in the centre, while the pulpit is part of the circle of surrounding seats, thereby giving a greater feeling of intimacy.

If you continue along the Boulevard François 1 you will come to the Fine Arts Museum. This is built entirely of glass and steel and has a roof specially designed to let in as much light as possible to the picture galleries. Two artists who painted in Normandy – nineteenth-century Eugène Boudin, forerunner of the Impressionists, and twentieth-century Raoul Dufy – are well-represented here.

If you next turn down the Boulevard Clemenceau, you will arrive back at the seafront. Incidentally, it is possible to do a boat trip round the harbour and even go over one of the great Atlantic liners. To do this, you will have to apply for information at the Syndicat d'Initiative, near the Town Hall.

The Seine from Le Havre to Rouen

The Seine, 776 km. long, rises in Burgundy and passes through Champagne, Île de France and Normandy to the sea. It flows through flat countryside, wooded or pastureland, and below tall cliffs, not unlike those along the coast. These heights, dropping sheer to the river, were sometimes crowned by castles such as Château Gaillard, while in the curving bends, where the river was deep, ports were sited, such as at Rouen.

Since early times, when a wooded countryside made travel difficult, this highway has linked Paris with the sea. In the Bronze Age, when tin was brought along the Seine from Cornwall to mix with copper, it was known as the Tin Road. From the sixth century, monasteries, centres of learning, were built beside the Seine, as well as small towns and settlements which during the ninth and tenth centuries produced rich booty for the plundering, pillaging Northmen. Later, after Rollo had made his treaty with Charles the Simple, it became one of the most civilized areas of France. The Normans, ashamed of their ravaging ancestors, outstripped all others in their generosity and support of the Church.

Today, although the Seine is highly industrialized with petrol refineries and factories along its banks, some of it is still picturesque, especially part of the drive along its banks between Le Havre and Rouen, a journey which takes about three hours. This can also be done by local bus, but should you decide to do this, see that the bus trip is *à bord de la Seine*, as there are two routes to Rouen. There is also a boat trip between June and September. This visits Honfleur (some also visit Trouville) on the other side of the estuary as well, the whole journey taking about ten and a half hours. The boat, the *Duc de Normandie*, leaves from the Quai de l'Yser, Le Havre.

The outskirts of Le Havre are ugly and sprawling. You will pass but not cross the new Tancarville bridge, the largest suspension bridge in Europe, linking Le Havre and the Caux promontory with the south side of the estuary. There is not much interesting to see until Lillebonne, and then only the shape of a Roman amphitheatre, a semi-circle of stone covered by grass, in its main square. Lillebonne was known as Juliabonne after a Roman proconsul, and was then an important port, but it is now silted up. It was here that William the Conqueror met his barons and planned the invasion of England.

After this comes a particularly ugly and smelly bit, the petrol refinery and factories of Port Jérôme. Things improve after Norville. First comes Villequier, situated at the foot of wooded hills, crowned by a castle. Then comes forest, and the river appears, very pleasant now, lined with nice old-timbered houses and gardens, backed by white cliffs, and Caudebec, with its attractive old church, built between 1475 and 1539, just visible through the trees. This delightful town and river resort was once the capital of the Caux region.

It was at Caudebec that, when a great tide was running, the sea entering the estuary met the river flow. The sea current reversed the stream one, causing a 'bore', an enormous tidal wave, which was most exciting to watch. However, special engineering work on the river banks has reduced the size of the bores and danger.

The abbey of St Wandrille is not far from here. This old ruin, founded in 649, has little of its abbey church left except a few tall Gothic pillars and the bases of columns which supported the main arches of the nave. However, the galleries of its cloisters, dating from the fourteenth and fifteenth centuries, are still in good condition. But only men are allowed inside.

St Wandrille is named after Wandrille, a wise and handsome count at Frankish King Dagobert's court. He was about to be married when both he and his bride decided that they would devote the rest of their lives to the service of God. The bride entered a convent and Wandrille, to the great despair and displeasure of his king, joined a group of hermits. He eventually went to St Ouen in Rouen, where he was ordained. Because of his magnificent physique, he was known as 'God's true athlete'.

When Wandrille founded the abbey, a stream, the Fontenelle, passed over the site, and it was first called after this. The Fontenelle library and school became a renowned centre of saintliness and learning. After being destroyed by the Northmen, it was restored in the tenth century, when it took the name of its founder, and became one of the most famous centres of the Benedictine Order. St Wandrille survived the wars of religion, but fell into ruins after the Revolution, when its monks had been dispersed. It passed through various hands, the Benedictines themselves returned in 1894 for a few years; the author, Maurice Maeterlinck, lived in the abbey for a while.

The monastery church to be seen there now is an old fifteenth-century tithe barn, which was transported from La Neville du Bosc in 1969, and is in use.

Le Trait, which has a lot of villas, is quite a pretty place, with an attractive grey-steepled church. Jumièges abbey nearby, beautifully situated on a bend of the Seine, one of France's greatest and loveliest ruins, is now under the supervision of the Fine Arts Department.

Jumièges abbey, founded by St Philibert from the Benedictine Order in the seventh century, and later destroyed by Northmen, was rebuilt by Duke William Longsword in the tenth century. Like St Wandrille it was also a centre of learning, but became so famous for its hospitality and charity that it became known as the Jumièges almshouse.

Its great glories are the roofless nave of the Church of Our Lady, where massive pillars and rounded arches rise to a height of 27 metres, and the delicate stonework of the transept and chancel. Charles vii, Jeanne d'Arc's king, often stayed at Jumièges with his favourite mistress, Agnes Sorel, who died there in 1450.

The Jumièges monks were dispersed at the Revolution and the abbey was sold at a public auction to a timber merchant. This vandal used it as a stone quarry, blowing up part of it, which accounts for the present ruin.

Du Clair is another riverside resort, but it is somehow more formal and solid than Caudebec. As one drives out of it, the chalk cliffs and wooded hills beyond are rather pretty. The river bends away again and the road runs through a picturesque wooded valley, then snakes through forests to Canteleu.

From this height there is a good view of the Seine river, Rouen and its busy port below. But the best view of Rouen is to be had from the Corniche de Rouen on the Mont Ste Cathérine, on the opposite side of the city.

Rouen

Rouen, the Ville Musée, which lies along the northern bank of the Seine, occupies a natural amphitheatre in the hills bordering this part of the Seine valley and is within easy reach by train of most of the Norman coastal resorts. I would recommend a day trip there rather than an overnight stay (unless booked beforehand); there is a chronic shortage of hotels in this popular tourist city, due chiefly to the number of old buildings in the centre.

Rouen, known as Ratuma by the Gauls, Rotomorgus by the Romans, and captured twice by the Northmen in the ninth century, became capital of the Norman duchy in 912. The Norse leader, Rollo, proved an able planner. His improvements to the river, narrowing and deepening the bed, linking islands with the mainland, and reinforcing the banks with quays, lasted until the nineteenth century.

It was at Rouen that John was supposed to have murdered Arthur, thus giving the French king, Philippe Auguste, the excuse to invade Normandy; the city was taken after an 80-day siege. The town prospered greatly during the following years, chiefly because of its good position and the trading pacts made first with Paris, then London, the Hanseatic cities, Flanders and Champagne. Rouen offered a stubborn resistance to the English Henry v, though he entered it in 1419; the city became French again when taken by Charles vii in 1449.

Much building took place during the period that followed, especially during the time of Cardinal d'Amboise (1460–1510), who introduced Renaissance architecture to Normandy. Although Rouen suffered badly during the Wars of Religion – it was sacked by the Protestants in 1562 – the Revocation of the Edict of Nantes was a worse disaster. After 1685 more than half its Protestant population, who were mostly employed in the textile industry, emigrated.

Like Le Havre, Rouen was badly bombed during the last war. Her famous cathedral and churches were badly damaged. The industrial district of St Sever and the area between the cathedral and the Seine were the worst hit.

The damage has now been repaired. St Sever has been rebuilt as a residential area and a university was built there in the 1960s. Rouen combines being an important industrial centre (especially for the spinning and weaving of cotton) and port with being Normandy's historic capital.

Rouen's most attractive feature is still its towers, spires, old streets and houses. Although bomb blast caused such havoc in the town centre, the houses' robust timber framing managed to withstand it, so that it was only the lath and plaster fillings which were blown to dust. As this has been put back and façades remounted, the intrinsic character of the streets still remains.

Many of these are so narrow that they are best explored on foot. Incidentally, for three francs you can get from the Syndicat d'Initiative (opposite the cathedral) an earpiece, which gives a commentary on the town in English.

For a tour of the town, the official guide starts from the Place du Vieux Marché, which is as good a place as any as you can leave your car there.

The Vieux Marché is a bit of a muddle, incorporating as it does a car park, a flower and food market (very useful for campers), as well as what looks like the beginning of an archaeological dig, and all surrounded by a mixture of old gabled houses and fairly new shops. A statue of Joan of Arc stands towards one end with fresh flowers either side. Nearby a plaque states that she was burned here on 30 May 1431, while another one shows the layout of the town at that time. Not far away a square of gilt mosaics claims to show the exact place where the pyre stood.

Jeanne d'Arc, about whom approximately 3,000 books have been written, occupies a curious position in French history. French armies and generals as esteemed as De Gaulle have been inspired by her; Napoleon, who was chiefly responsible for her re-interment about 1803, was another. After the First World War she was appropriated by the Right Wing as a symbol of national renewal. During the Occupation, she was used by the Germans as propaganda against the English, and became the symbol of the Collaborationists. Then, although she undoubtedly existed, that she was burned at the stake is now questioned. There is a museum to her in the Tour Jeanne d'Arc, a remnant of the old castle, which contains waxwork scenes from her life.

At the end of the square is the Rue de la Pie in which stands the rather grim house and birthplace of the author, Pierre Corneille (1606–84), now a museum of books and manuscripts. Rouen also has a museum to the writer, Gustave Flaubert (1821–80), who was born in its old hospital, where his father worked as a surgeon.

The Rue du Gros Horloge with its gabled and beamed houses, leading out of the Vieux Marché, is Rouen's best known and most picturesque street.

The great clock, very colourful in red, blue and gold, looking down at you, is the city's most popular landmark. Notice the rat (or is it a mouse?) at the end of the hour hand. There is a clock face either side. Needless to say, neither of them work.

The clock was originally in the belfry on one side, built in 1389, but to make it more conspicuous the townspeople had it incorporated into the arch, built in 1525.

The Rue du Gros Horloge leads out about opposite Notre Dame, which is considered to be one of the finest Gothic cathedrals in France. Its exterior bristles with intricate carvings, although it is badly in need of the repairs which it is at present undergoing.

The cathedral's main features are its two towers and spire, all quite different, yet somehow in harmony. The tower on the left, that of St Romanus, is squarish and plain, while the one on the right, the Butter Tower, is flamboyant and intricately carved. This last-mentioned got its name because its construction was financed by the sale of indulgences, which allowed devout people to eat butter and drink milk during Lent. It was never completed and was crowned not with a spire, but with an octagon, inside which is a carillon of 55 bells. Between these two towers soars the delicate open-ironwork spire, which at 151 metres is the tallest in France.

Rouen cathedral was constructed mainly in the thirteenth century after a devastating fire in 1200 which destroyed most of the eleventh- and twelfth-century building. Parts of it, such as the library, the very fine carved stone staircase and the Butter Tower were added in the fifteenth century; the spire was added in the nineteenth. In the eleventh-century crypt are the tombs of Richard Lionheart, dukes of Normandy and Georges d'Amboise, the Cardinal Minister of Louis XII.

After the cathedral St Maclou and St Ouen are Rouen's two next monumental treasures. If you leave the cathedral by the north transept door, you will emerge into a narrow alleyway, the Cour des Libraires (Booksellers' Court), which winds down to the Rue de la République, then to the square in front of St Maclou.

St Maclou is a masterpiece of flamboyant Gothic and has a magnificent five-gabled portal and carved wooden doorway. Like the cathedral – though this time in wood – it has a fine carved staircase (1517) to one side of a rather beautiful organ loft. Its spire was added in 1868.

After St Maclou find, if you can, the St Maclou cloister, down the side-turning beside the cathedral. There is an old fountain in the courtyard. The frieze of skulls and bones round the wooden beams of the surrounding building refers to a plague. Places get adapted and used in Rouen (like the Renaissance Bourgthéroulde mansion, just off the Vieux Marché, which has become a bank): these cloisters, most appropriately, house an art school.

Then take the Rue Damiette, a quaint old street which will lead into the Rue des Boucheries St Ouen, and to St Ouen itself, an excellent example of later Gothic. This church is particularly renowned for its beautiful and harmonious interior, an effect created by slender delicate shafts and an absence of ornate decorations. Its organ is one of the finest in France. There is a magnificent rose window on the south transept side. The central tower over the transept (1490–1515) ends in an octagonal lantern, which is known as the ducal crown of Normandy.

Rouen has some good museums. The museum of Fine Arts has a splendid collection of local pottery and ceramics, and a very fine picture gallery, including early Flemish artists, Italians and seventeenth-, eighteenth- and nineteenth-century French painters, particularly those with Norman associations. There is also an important collection of Impressionists. The Musée le Secq specializes in wrought iron (third to nineteenth centuries), which is displayed in the church of St Laurent and the museum of jewels and religious treasures is in the old Visitandines Convent.

For trips round the port and to La Bouille you get tickets from Transport Joffet at the Gar Routière.

9. Eure

Eure, lying astride the Lower Seine, is Normandy's most wooded department. More than a fifth of its surface is covered in trees, forming shaded forests, so pleasant to walk in and explore.

Normans here live chiefly by agriculture, producing wheat, dairy products and cider. The towns are small. Most people live in sleepy villages, their houses grouped picturesquely round a tall, grey, steepled church. Eure's peaceful prosperity and easy access of Paris has attracted many Parisians to buy weekend homes here, or to commute daily to Paris.

There are a few châteaux – Beaumesnil, Acquigny, and Champs de Bataille spring to mind – but you will see more tall manor houses, their timber-framed storeys mounted on stone blocks and surrounded by massive farm buildings, which bear witness to the general well-being of this region.

The drive south from Rouen along the Seine to Vernon, which takes about three hours, is quite interesting, but not so good as the drive the other way. Moreover, this time the local bus rarely goes near the river, so, if you use public transport, the journey is quicker and better by train.

If driving, two places to visit en route are the Deux Amants hill, about $4\frac{1}{2}$ km. from Amfreville sous les Monts (D20), and castle Gaillard at Les Andelys.

Deux Amants hill is renowned for its magnificent views over the Seine and the legend of how it got its name.

This story was first told in the twelfth century by Marie de France, France's first woman writer. The king of the Pitrois had a beautiful daughter, named Caliste. Perhaps he needed a strong son-in-law to succeed him. More likely, he just didn't want his daughter to marry. At any rate, he forbade her to accept any man unless he could carry her at the run to the top of the hill. Raoul, her favourite, did his best to succeed, but alas, the strain was too great. When he at last reached the top, he dropped dead from exhaustion. The heart-broken Caliste died, too, almost immediately afterwards. So, the two ill-fated young lovers were buried where they fell. The exact place, I'm afraid, is not known, but their epitaph is romantically immortalized in the name of the hill.

One's first sight of Les Andelys is of its castle, looming white and gaunt, as if growing out of the chalky cliffside. You can take a car most of the way up to it, but the last bit, a fairly stiff climb, has to be done on foot.

Château Gaillard is one of Normandy's most attractive ruins, but is just to be looked at and scrambled over, although the guide there will try and charge you a franc if he can.

In its heyday it incorporated everything known to twelfth-century military architects, and Richard the Lionheart had picked up quite a bit of information from his campaigns in Palestine. He had every reason to be proud of his 'year-old daughter', although the story that it was actually built in a year is now disputed. There is evidence that it was built between 1195 and 1198.

After Richard's death, Philippe first took the fortresses at Lyons, Gournay, Conches and Verneuil before laying siege to Gaillard in August 1203. The castle, defended by Roger de Lasci, Constable of Chester, although short of food and munitions, withstood it until 6 March 1204. Even then, it was only taken by a ruse. A soldier, so the story goes, climbed in through the latrines and let down the drawbridge. After its capture, the other Norman fortresses capitulated, and Normandy became part of France.

It has held some distinguished prisoners, such as Marguerite of Burgundy, who was imprisoned there by King Louis x, along with her two sisters, in 1314. The king, wishing to be free to marry again, accused her of adultery. The unfortunate queen is supposed to have been strangled in her chamber with her own hair. The fortress changed hands many times during the Hundred Years' War. It was besieged for two years by Henri IV during the Wars of Religion. When it finally fell, he had it dismantled. Some of its stones were used in the construction of other buildings, one of which was the Convent of the Capucins at Andelys.

There is a magnificent view of the town, the leafy valley and curling Seine with its island and graceful new suspension bridge from the castle, although this is perhaps somewhat marred by the smoking factory chimneys of the new industrial Grand Andelys on the right. The Petit Andelys, nearest the river, most fortunately undamaged by the war, has an attractive square of old houses and plane trees with the sturdy twelfth-century church of St Sauveur to one side. Most of the Grand Andelys was destroyed in June 1940, but its sixteenth-century Notre Dame church, a mixture of Flamboyant Gothic and Renaissance, is still worth visiting. Nicolas Poussin (1594–1665), Normandy's most famous painter, was born at Villiers-sur-Andely, not far from here.

Vernon, situated either side of the Seine between the forests of Bizy and Vernon, is a pleasant relaxing town with a number of fine avenues and many of the amenities of a seaside resort. The best view of it is from its bridge – ruined piles of the old twelfth-century bridge, with the castle tower which was once joined to it, lie to one side.

Vernon, one of the gates to Normandy, was supposed to have been founded by Rollo, but old documents show that it had a charter in 750. Its position made it of strategic importance during the Middle Ages, when it became a favourite place to stay of both English and French kings. Louis IX (1214–1270), always known in French history as St Louis, because he was so pious, was a well-known visitor here, especially in hot weather.

Unfortunately, many of Vernon's old wooden houses in the centre were destroyed in the last war, so that there is not much old to see now, other than its twelfth-century collegiate church and a few old houses near by. The church has a beautiful nave and rose window (west front). But don't waste time looking for the six Louis XIII tapestries, as they were stolen at the end of 1972.

One of the loveliest places to visit in Eure is the beautiful beech and oak forest of Lyons, once a favourite hunting ground of the Dukes of Normandy, when it covered an area considerably larger than its present 26,500 acres. Experts from all over the world come to study its trees and the silviculture practised. Some beeches and oaks grow to an enormous size in this chalky soil. One great beech, known as God's Beech, is 275 years old, and has a circumference of more than 14 feet. One great oak is 300 years old.

Winding roads lead down to the village of Lyons, lying in a deep valley in the heart of this forest. It is pretty, peaceful and old with its eighteenth-century market place and 15th-century church. As it has several hotels, you could choose few better inland places to stay for a few days.

Lyons is best approached from Andelys, passing Lisors, or from Fleury-sur-Andelle, or, if coming from Rouen, via Vascoeuil.

Evreux, situated around the many arms of the Iton river, is Eure's capital. To me it will always be a city of water. The first time I stayed there, my hotel window opened dangerously out over a narrow noisy stream. Then everywhere were little stone bridges and brooks. The cathedral and bishop's palace, a delightful ensemble enclosed within walls covered in foliage, added their greenery to the weedy water below. A pretty walk, the Promenade des Ramparts to the left of the cathedral, leads past a moat, beside which benches have been built into the Gallo-Roman ramparts. Within a few minutes one can escape the city's noise.

Evreux, as the centre of a rich agricultural region and with plenty of small industries, is cheerful, active and bustling. At present, it is difficult to drive through, but will be less so when the ring road planned to divert the N13 Paris–Deauville traffic from the centre is built.

It has plenty of history, being both a Gallic and Roman capital, and having had a more than fair share of sackings and burnings – Normans in the ninth century, English Henry 1 in 1119, French Philippe Auguste in 1193, French Jean the Good in 1356. A further French king, Charles v, laid siege to it in 1379. In 1940 the city blazed for nearly a week after German air raids. The raids of 1944 were even more catastrophic.

Because of the town's hectic past Notre Dame cathedral shows a mixture of styles, dating from the eleventh to the eighteenth centuries. You should enter it through the Flamboyant Gothic north door, with its richly designed stone lacework. The interior is high and white: the great arches of the nave being the only part remaining of the original church. Note especially the stained glass windows; those of the apse are considered to be one of the best examples of fourteenth-century glass. Note also the wood carving of the ambulatory chapel. The screen to the fourth chapel is particularly outstanding.

The bishop's palace, next door to the cathedral, now houses a museum, which has a good collection of Gallo-Roman and medieval remains.

The former abbey church of St Taurinus, the first bishop of Evreux in the fourth century, is worth looking at. It was built during the fourteenth and fifteenth centuries and among its treasures it boasts St Taurinus' shrine, a gift to hold St Taurinus' relic from the French king, St Louis, to the abbey in the thirteenth century. Ornately carved, a masterpiece of craftsmanship, and in the shape of a miniature chapel, this silver gilt reliquary was probably made locally. It was wisely hidden away during the Revolution.

Evreux, situated about halfway between Paris and the coast, makes a good stopping place and is also a good centre for further excursions.

Louviers, about 20 km. to the north is worth visiting, if only to see its church of Notre Dame, most fortunately undamaged by the surrounding bombing. In any case, its exterior, especially the south wall, is so exuberantly flamboyant and covered with so much ornamentation, that probably a few missing decorations would not be noticed. Many works of art decorate the walls of its elegant thirteenth-century nave.

To the west of Louviers lies the famous old abbey of Bec-Hellouin, which is still in use. Its fifteenth-century St Nicholas

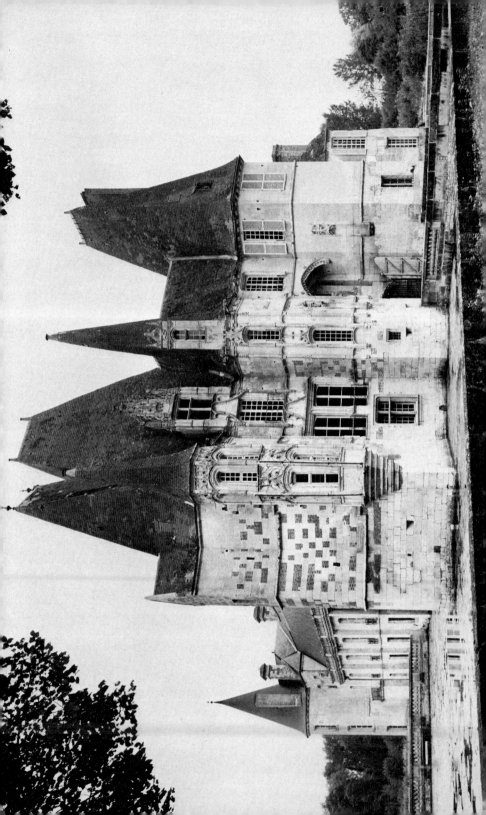

Tower, 45 metres high, a landmark for miles, is the chief reminder of the abbey's past.

In the Middle Ages Bec-Hellouin was a renowned religious and cultural centre. The abbey got its name from a knight called Herluin, who in 1034 exchanged his charger for a donkey and took a vow to devote his life to God. Within about ten years, many others had joined him here in the Bec valley.

Some quite illustrious people were attracted to stay there, such as Lanfranc in 1042, who later became the trusted friend and adviser of William the Conqueror and Archbishop of Canterbury, an office attained by another of Bec's abbots, Anselm, in 1093.

The first abbey, founded by Herluin, was at Bonneville Appetot, but was moved farther up the valley in 1060. It was fortified by Louis Harcourt, governor of Normandy in 1336, damaged by the English during the Hundred Years' War, and by the Protestants in the Wars of Religion. The monks were driven out during the Revolution and the great abbey church was demolished during the time of Napoleon.

Today, only the column foundations of the old abbey remain. The refectory, a majestically proportioned and vaulted hall constructed between 1742 and 1747, now houses the new abbey, which has been occupied by Benedictines since 1948.

Vernueil-sur-Avre, about 43 km. to the west of Evreux and a rather distinguished-looking little town, is descended from a fortified city created in the twelfth century by Henry I when duke of Normandy. Along with Tillières and Nonnancourt it formed part of the Avre defence line against the French king's army.

Today, Vernueil's most attractive feature is the tower of Ste Magdalène's church, 56 metres high and rising in three tiers, crowned by an octagonal lantern. Massive yet delicately carved, it is more magnificent in some ways than the Butter Tower at Rouen. The church, a slightly older sixteenth-century Renaissance structure, suffered some war damage, and its interior, restored rather badly in the last century, is disappointing.

Notre Dame church, lying in a tangle of narrow streets, is difficult to see properly, but has an interior more attractive than the

23 *Château d'O, the entrance front*

reddish stone twelfth-century, but much restored, exterior. The many early sixteenth-century statues inside were mostly carved by local sculptors.

To the east of Notre Dame still stands the stout circular Tour Grise, built by Henri 1 to protect the town. The north side of Vernueil, near the Hotel de Ville and Rond-point de la Victoire has adapted the old to the new. A shaded park has been made on the hill, which must once have been part of the outer ramparts and which slopes down to the river, once a moat.

10. Orne

The Orne is predominantly a hilly country and especially so in the west, where the countryside is broken and wooded and the farmland a patchwork of hedged enclosures. Its two highest points, the Signal d'Ecouves and Mont Avaloirs, both 417 metres, are also the highest in western France. Eastwards lie the flatter plains of Alençon and Argentan, where much wheat is grown.

Like Eure, Orne is chiefly a pastoral country, famed for its cattle and dairy produce. From the north-east, in the Auge region, comes Camembert cheese, perfected by Marie Harel at the beginning of the nineteenth century and named after the village where it was first made, near Vimoutiers. In the east is the Perche, the birthplace of a famous breed of draught horses, the Normandy Percheron.

Today, the chief area for horse-breeding lies between l'Aigle, an old industrial town, once renowned for its production of pins and needles, and Argentan.

Argentan to Alençon

Argentan lies on the plain between the Ecouves forest and the Gouffern woodland, which was where the final battle of Normandy took place in August 1944. The town was so badly damaged in the fighting that it has been almost completely rebuilt, so there is little interesting to see there now.

Even when I visited it, nearly 30 years later, the old church of St Germanus was still undergoing repairs and restoration and was closed to the public. Argentan was once famous for its lace. Although you can still see specimens in the Benedictine Abbey (1, Rue de l'Abbaye), it is no longer made.

However, Argentan is not far from two places of interest, Le Pin-au-Haras and the Château d'O.

The Pin stud, fortunately undamaged in the fighting, lies on the main road RN24*bis*, near Argentan. This fine building, lying at the end of the long Avenue Louis XIV and surrounded by 3,000 acres of woodland and pastures has a lordly and magnificent air as befits some of the aristocratic creatures bred there. You could call it the Horses' Versailles, as indeed it was designed by Jules Hardouin Mansart, the same architect who was responsible for Louis XIV's grand palace. The main courtyard, the Cour Colbert, is named after that king's minister, who laid the foundation of this and many other successful projects.

The main building, the château, built 1717–28, is the residence of the manager, while the 100 stallions – English thoroughbreds, French trotters, hacks, Anglo-Arabs, Norman cobs and Percherons, are kept in the stables in the wings. At one time, Le Pin was the principal nursery of horses for the army. It is now primarily a Stud Officers' Training School.

For anyone interested in horses, it is a great sight to see them all departing and returning from their daily exercise. The stud is open from 9 till noon and 2 to 6 every day. Entrance is free. A groom will show you round. There is an annual steeplechase on the second Sunday in October at Le Pin racecourse, and the annual meeting, including flat racing and steeplechasing, is on the first Sunday in August.

For anyone interested in horse riding, a very pleasant way to explore the woodlands and meadows of Orne is by horse. All-inclusive package holidays are available, excluding beginners – weekends, 250 frs: 3 or 4 days' riding 435 or 612 frs: a week, 965 frs. For details, apply to the Association Départementale de Tourisme Equestre et d'Equitation de Loisirs de l'Orne, 60 Grande Rue, 61–Alençon, France.

Château d'O, not far from Le Pin-au-Haras is famous for its

curious name and strange appearance, especially its fifteenth-century east side. Neither a house nor a castle, it is a mixture of narrow sloping roofs, steeples, turrets and gables. Château d'O, built out of plain rose brick, consists of three buildings surrounding three sides of a courtyard and overlooking a moat lake. The central part, with its tall windows, was added in the sixteenth century. Slim columns supporting its arcade are decorated with ermine carvings, the emblem of the house of O. The west side, rebuilt in the eighteenth century, is the living quarters.

Unfortunately, the château grounds are closed between 1 July and 10 September, and the castle is not open at all. So the visitor is only able to admire its grand and graceful structure, so attractively reflected in the water.

If you drive to Mortrée from here, then take the N158, you will arrive at the old cathedral town of Sées, the seat of Orne's bishopric, and not far from the source of the Orne river.

But Sées, in spite of its grand ecclesiastical past is now just a small town which has seen better days, with little streets leading to its cathedral. An air of seedy shabbiness hangs over it.

Sées, the Sagium of Roman times and a bishopric from the fourth century, was supposed to have been founded by a colony of Saxons. Its cathedral, St Latriun, was destroyed many times by the Northmen, and the present one, a good example of Norman Gothic, was built in the thirteenth and fourteenth centuries.

It is shaped like a vast Latin cross, 106 metres long. The decorations and stained glass windows are best over the chancels and transepts. Most of the stained glass windows tell stories, which are explained in notices below, a great help to sightseers. The high window glass disappeared in the Wars of Religion, in 1573.

Fortunately Our Lady of Sées, a white marble statue decorated with gold in the south transept, managed to escape all the pillages of the cathedral during the fourteenth century, in 1450, 1556, and especially in 1793. She has a most intriguing air of *songerie* (dreaminess) as she gazes down at her child, who holds an orange, the world, in one hand.

In spite of the town's past, its seminaries and monasteries and churches, there is very little to see in Sées, apart from its cathedral. True, there is a small museum near by in the square, but it is not a very important one. The old bishops' palace at the east end of the cathedral looked almost dilapidated behind its fine wrought-iron gates. In any case, it now houses offices.

The Château de Carrouges, one of Normandy's most famous castles, lies about 26 km. to the west of Sées. Unlike that of O it can be visited.

Huge, ornate, square and surrounded by a moat, it too is made of rose red brick. Carrouges' most famous features are its elegant, ornate, wrought-iron gates, made by Jean Goujon, at the end of the terrace at the entrance front. Inside, the house also has a very fine stairway. The state rooms are decorated in a mixture of Renaissance and classical styles, combining simplicity with splendour, and provide a rich background to the furniture. The portrait gallery is most interesting.

Carrouges was built between the thirteenth and seventeenth centuries, but mostly during the sixteenth and seventeenth in the reign of Henri IV, to replace a fortress built above the village at the top of a hill. The castle was owned by the Tillières family, a well-known Norman one, and Lords of Carrouges from the twelfth century.

If you have a car you should make the drive from Sées to Alençon through the forest of Ecouves, whose stretch of trees – oak, beech, pine and spruce – is reckoned to be one of the loveliest in France. Take the N808, then after 'Les Choux', at Carrefour de la Range, take the D226 on the left.

Although the area called Ecouves Forest is about 37,000 acres, much of it is scrub, moorland and pastures. The best bit, the real forest, only about 20,000 acres, which is state property, lies in the centre. Roads, tracks and lanes cut through it. Ecouves is renowned for its mushrooms, fishing, wild boar and deer hunting, reserved for members of the appropriate organizations, of course. Also, the variety of its insects, especially beetles. In summer walkers should beware of vipers.

Once hunted over by Norman nobles, Ecouves forest was appropriated to the French crown by Philippe Auguste in 1220. Some centuries later, Colbert, under Louis XIV, gave the use of part of the forest to glass-blowers, an industry which prospered there up to the end of the eighteenth century. In 1790, it became state property. The last war saw its greatest drama when it was the scene of the battle between the division commanded by the French general, LeClerc, and the entrenched Germans, who had taken refuge there.

A tank now stands at Croix de Médavy to commemorate this important battle and the men of the French 2nd Division, who cleared the forest of Germans on 12 and 13 August 1944. The viewpoint at this crossroads is marked by an old milestone, carved with old road names.

From here, you take the road towards Croix Madame, another viewpoint, and in the centre of the most attractive part of the forest. In fact, you should get out here and explore some of the walks on foot. That along the Sapie Pichon path is the best. If you drive down the D204 to the Vignage rocks crossroads, then bear right to the D26, you will eventually reach Alençon. The Vignage rocks are another and more attractive viewpoint over the forest. A walk to them takes about three-quarters of an hour, there and back.

Alençon, situated around the Sarthe and Riante rivers, and capital of the Orne Department, had the distinction of being the first town in France to be liberated by General Leclerc. The French 2nd Division entered it on 12 August, and on the 13th cut the Paris–Granville road at Ecouché. On the 19th the Poles (1st Canadian Army) and Americans cut off the German 7th Army retreat at Chambois, near Le Pin-au-Haras (a stele marks the place) and forced them to surrender. By 21 August the battle of Normandy was over.

Alençon fortunately escaped much damage and has retained her old monuments, houses and streets. Even so, I was not very impressed when I first saw the town. Like Sées, it appeared bitty, seedy and run-down. However, it is a town that grows on you, and I ended up by liking it, and would have liked to have spent longer exploring it.

Because of its position on so many roads, it is a town that visitors to France are likely to find themselves passing through on the way somewhere else. Anyone with time to spare would probably enjoy a few hours looking round.

The best place to start on a tour of Alençon is the Place Foch, because you can park your car there. Also, here stand the old palace of the dukes, the bridge, the Palace of Justice and Hôtel de Ville, all making an attractive ensemble and very photogenic, especially when seen from the little garden past the bridge.

Alençon on the border of Normandy, and once known as the city of the dukes, has had quite a long and bloodthirsty history. It was captured by William the Conqueror in 1048, but the oldest parts of the castle to be seen now are its fifteenth-century pepper-pot tower and fortified gateway. Today the castle houses a prison, and probably always will do, I was told. Between 1940 and 1944 many arrested French patriots were martyred within its grim walls by the Gestapo, either by execution on the spot or by dispatch to extermination camps.

The museum in the Town Hall opposite is chiefly one of paintings and would be of interest to anyone keen on French painters, such as Jouvenet, Rigaud, Chardin, Boudin, Courbet, and Géricault, but there are no Impressionists. It also holds a collection of lace, for which Alençon has long been well-known.

The bridge past the little garden leads to the Promenade des Rosaires, a park which contains a few animals – a donkey, goats, deer – which children might enjoy feeding. There are also some peacocks, those fine actors, who can usually be relied upon to put on a show and display their fine tails. Behind this is a pretty garden and aviary.

The Grande Rue, a mere rather narrow street, is Alençon's main thoroughfare and contains some quaint old houses. The interesting little well you will see (the Syndicat d'Initiative did not know the date) with steps inside a tower doesn't really belong there, but is a transplant from somewhere else 'because it fills the space rather nicely'.

The famous church of Notre Dame, fourteenth-century Flamboyant Gothic, seems to plunge straight down into the road, so that one has to walk backwards in the street opposite to see it properly. It is particularly renowned for its three-sided porch, very flamboyant and intricately carved. Christ stands in the centre, while John stands beneath him, his back turned unexpectedly to the street.

Inside, about the first thing you will notice is the sanctuary to Ste Thérèse, probably ablaze with candles. The stained glass windows above show her baptism in the church here with the words, *Sancta Thérèse ora pro nobis* below.

Ste Thérèse, whose full name was Marie Françoise Thérèse Martin, was born in Alençon in 1873, one of nine sisters. You can visit her home and see her birthroom, and there is a chapel dedicated to her in the Rue St Blaise, just off the Grande Rue.

Her father was a watchmaker and her mother a laceworker. Both were extremely pious and before they were married had both tried unsuccessfully to enter a religious establishment. Because of this it is not too surprising that Thérèse entered a convent when only 15.

She was, I suppose, a rather neurotic girl, who suffered badly from feelings of guilt, which she managed to hide under a pleasant and smiling exterior, doing good deeds, so that no one would have suspected her inner turmoil. She contracted tuberculosis and died painfully when only 24. It was the *Histoire d'une âme* ('History of a soul') – papers describing her feelings and experiences – which made her name. This work was first published in 1898, then after extensive revisions again in 1956. She was canonized in 1925 and in 1945 was named the second patroness of France after Ste Jeanne. Her feast day is October 3.

As well as being the birthplace of Ste Thérèse, Alençon is France's chief source of lace. You can visit the School of Lace in the Pont Neuf, a street just opposite the Syndicat d'Initiative in the Grande Rue. Ring the bell. The people here are usually glad to show visitors round.

However, you can no longer watch the laceworkers at work, as there are very few of them now. You can only see the famous collection. For 2.50 francs a voice in English will guide you round the rooms, although as the loudspeaker is in the first room, you have to listen rather hard when you enter the other two. Triumphant music accompanies these speeches.

It is a great pity that Alençon lace is likely to die out soon, because it is very lovely. But it is difficult now to find people willing to do this intricate and painstaking work. They can only work three hours a day at it. A small piece can take up to 68 hours to make. Only in Brussels and Alençon is lace still made by hand.

The collection is extremely rich, containing the beautiful Pointe d'Alençon veil worn by Marie Antoinette, while some of the lace is so delicate that it has to be looked at under a magnifying glass. Lace-making in Alençon is due to that indefatigable minister, Colbert, who, to help the town prosper, financed the making of lace here. In 1665, it was decreed that no more lace be imported into France from abroad.

In the showroom, you can buy pieces of exquisite lace – at a price! A tiny square costs about £13. A little cheaper are dolls with lace caps and cuffs, about £6. The hankies, trimmed with lace, come a little cheaper still, at about £3 each.

Alençon makes a good centre for excursions. Apart from the Ecouves forest to the north, it is within easy reach of the Perseigne forest to the south-east. To the west lie the Marcelles Alps, hardly mountains, but attractively steep, heather-covered hills enclosing the Sarthe valley. Farther west still lies Bagnoles-sur-Orne.

Bagnoles-sur-Orne

Bagnoles-sur-Orne, so picturesquely situated around a lake and surrounded by forest, must be the only spa in the world whose medicinal waters were discovered by a horse.

Exactly when it happened is somewhat obscure. But the story goes that a knight named Hugues de Tessé was too tender-hearted to put his faithful horse, Rapide, to death when he got old and senile. Instead, he bid him sadly goodbye, then let him loose in the Andaine forest.

Time passed. Then, one day, to his utter amazement, Rapide returned to his stable. But he was no longer a worn-out, old horse. He was a new, lively, rejuvenated Rapide. What had happened?

Tessé determined to solve the mystery and tracked his hoof marks, back through the forest. They led to a spring in which the horse had apparently bathed. Tessé bathed, too, and found to his delight that he also felt young again.

From that time onwards, Bagnoles was known as a place of healing and rejuvenation. One Capucin monk is even supposed to have become so randy that he made a 13ft leap from one rocky spur to another. This place is now known as the Capucin's leap.

Today, Bagnoles is a spa resort, chiefly for diseases of the circulation, gynaecological problems, and also for fractures from accidents. Its sulphuric salt waters are to be bathed in, not taken. Whether or not they do really possess all the curative powers claimed, I don't know, but it is such a pleasant, peaceful place, that a few days spent there would make anyone feel better.

Bagnoles used to be very popular with English and American visitors, but since the war few of them come here. This is rather remarkable as it is such a delightful place to stay and would make a pleasant break of a few days during a long journey through France. There are plenty of good hotels and restaurants.

A village of some sort or another has probably existed around the lakeside since early times. Its waters have long been used for bathing in, although the early baths here were very rough and ready. The place did not become really important until the nineteenth century, when a rich American, a Mr Gould, invested money in it. He built a casino and the large red-shuttered hotel beside the lake, which is now let out in apartments.

There are now two casinos, both overlooking the lake and open from the beginning of May to the end of September. The biggest casino, which includes a cinema and dance hall, was built by Mr Gould. The other one belongs to a family but has been recently bought by the town, which intends to improve it, so it should be open by 1974.

Apart from the casinos you can sit on one of the many seats

dotted around the lakeside, listen to the birds, or watch the swans glide over the water. Or, if you feel energetic, you can take out a white pedalo boat (a bit expensive though at three francs for a quarter of an hour). You can stroll round the town, which has some good shops, or explore one of the many forest walks.

The Hôtel des Thermes, on the edge of the town, can be reached from any of the hotels by a little bus which runs between Bagnoles station and Tessé church, every afternoon between 2 p.m. and 6.45. The Hôtel stands beside the road in a natural park, backed by rocks, gushing streams and forest paths. I met a woman who had been coming there for 22 years to bathe her legs, a treatment which she can get partly financed by the French equivalent of our National Health Scheme.

The best view of Bagnoles is to be had from the Roc au Chien. This rather blunt-faced dog is approached up the Sentier de l'Avenir and stone staircase, nearly opposite the Casino in the Avenue du Château. Turn left, and you eventually come to three posts. Not far down on the left fork is the left-hand path leading to this rocky projection. From it, you have a very clear view of the forest, Bagnoles, and the lake.

Bagnoles is an excellent centre for excursions. Near at hand is Tessé la Madeleine with its Château de la Roche Bagnoles, Renaissance in style, but built by a rich old lady about 1850, and now the Town Hall. If you buy an eight-franc book of tickets from the Syndicat d'Initiative, you can, amongst other things, attend concerts, visit exhibitions, the little cinema and take trips on the miniature railway. Further afield is the Zoological Park at St Symphorien des Monts (bus from Bagnoles every Tuesday), also the enchanted village at Bellefontaine, a park catering particularly for children. Both these two places are in Manche.

If you have no car or feel like a rest from driving, you can go on one of the many organized bus tours. There are two companies, Normandie Excursions and Les Circuits Bagnolais. You can visit Swiss Normandy, or even go as far as Mont St Michel. Prices range from 16 to 19 francs, which is reasonable considering the distance covered. However, these buses are small (they seat only

about 22 people), comfortable and very popular, so that you need
to book at least a day ahead.

Swiss Normandy

Swiss Normandy, shaped by the Orne cutting its way through the
Armorican Massif, is one of the most attractive areas of Normandy, especially popular with walkers, anglers, canoeists and
campers.

It is a region of deep gorges, high rocky cliffs, wooded valleys
and occasional peaks from which to view the rolling countryside.
Although it does not possess high mountains or lakes, you could
call it a Switzerland in miniature.

Most of it lies in Calvados and its nearest large town is Falaise.
However, I am putting it in at the end of the Orne chapter as it
makes such a good trip from Bagnoles.

Ferté Macé, the first town you pass, is also a spa, and quite
attractive with a large church. It is noted for its tripe cooked on
skewers. Briouze, the next one, is famous for its cheese. After crossing the bridge at Forêt Auvray Pont, the road snakes down a wild,
tree-covered valley, difficult to drive down quickly. It is very
peaceful and hard to imagine swarming with soldiers as it was 30
years ago, when Montgomery's troops fought their way through
this area.

Swiss Normandy's most famous viewpoint is the one from Roche
d'Oëtre, which overlooks the deep valley of the Rouve through
which this stream twists and turns between slopes massed with
trees. Around another path near by is the Profil Humain, the outline of a rocky face with quite a sensitive nose. Although there is no
charge for visiting the rocks, they form part of a café's grounds and
you are supposed to buy some little souvenir there. These are quite
nice – pottery, cheese, slippers, dolls, nuts, sweets, cards, etc.

Clécy, a large village, lying around a curve of the Orne, is the
centre of Swiss Normandy and a place from which walkers start on
their explorations. You can visit its folklore museum in a sixteenth-
century manor house, climb to the top of the Sugar Loaf rock for a

good view, or cross the bridge to Vey on the other side of the river. The Hostellerie du Moulin du Vey, situated so picturesquely beside the river, waterfalls and rocks, serves food and drinks, but would probably be expensive to stay at, also noisy because of the turning wheels and waterfalls. There is also a cider cellar at Clécy, which you can visit for a franc, including drinks of cider afterwards. You can also buy bottles of cider here and take a ride on the miniature railway through the Parc de Loisirs.

After Clécy, you can go on to Thury Harcourt, a pleasant tourist centre on the northern edge of Swiss Normandy, or return to Bagnoles via Condé sur Noireau, descending through forests past flint quarries to Pont Erambourg, and down the valley of the Vire to Flers. Flers, a rather grey nondescript town, boasts a fine sixteenth-century château, now a Town Hall and museum, partly surrounded by a moat and with a simple but attractive garden.

You could next visit Domfront, spread out along a rocky crest, once a strongly fortified border town. From the terrace of the public gardens made out of the old castle ruins is a splendid view of the river Varenne and the last wooded hills of lower Normandy.

11. Calvados

The Calvados, the department most visited by English tourists, is also the one which has played the most important part in our island history. Even its name, Calvados, is supposed to have come from a ship of the Spanish Armada, the *Salvador*, which after the defeat of 1588, while making for home, foundered on a reef near Arromanches.

Its highest part lies in the Swiss Normandy of the south-west; elsewhere it is low-lying, but varied, especially its coastline, with stretches of cliffs, reefs, and sands backed by dunes and marshes. The damp mild climate and rich soils of the hinterlands, the Pays d'Auge and Bessin, provide rolling hills of lush pastures and apple orchards. Most of the Campagne de Caen and Lieuvin is devoted to fields of wheat, sugar beet and apple orchards. Scattered among the cultivated fields between Caen and Falaise are stone quarries, the stone for which Caen has been famous for centuries. Later discoveries of iron ore led to the building of steelworks around Caen.

Falaise

Falaise, which has so many links with Britain, is still an attractive city in spite of the cruel destruction of the last war. Its rugged castle, birthplace of William the Conqueror, still stands on its high crag overlooking the town, set in the rocky Ante valley.

This stronghold, a tour of which takes about an hour, is reckoned to be one of the oldest in Normandy. Its history is long and exciting. It is sufficient to say here that it has endured many sieges, especially during the Hundred Years' War, and changed hands several times during the Wars of Religion. In 1589, after its thick walls had been bombarded and broken by Henri iv's artillery, it was dismantled and abandoned for about 200 years. However, it came back into use again in the eighteenth century, when the Town Hall was erected in its grounds, and in the nineteenth a college was built where the garrison barracks had stood.

Falaise castle came back properly into its own again during the Second World War when its Talbot Tower was used by the Germans as an observation post and the college assembly hall as a field bakery. During the furious battle that raged round it in mid-August 1944, machine-guns were fired through its windows at Montgomery's troops on the Caen road.

The castle and the town's monuments have now been restored from the débâcle that followed and are worth looking at, if only for their legends and their historical interest.

There is the Arlette fountain below the castle, and which once stood amongst old tanneries in a quaint area destroyed during the war. Today, two towers, a bas-relief and inscription mark the place where the 18-year-old Duke Robert was supposed to have first met the girl, Arlette.

However, as his castle window overlooked the stream, as she probably well knew, they had probably seen each other often before that fine spring evening in 1027, as told in the poem by Benoît de Sainte-Maure, Chronicler of the Duchy of Normandy, and written at the request of Henri ii.

Duke Robert, younger son of Richard ii, was returning home from the hunt when he saw this beautiful girl washing her linen in the stream. He didn't waste much time. Shortly afterwards, his chamberlain was sent to her father, Herbert, a well-to-do tanner, to demand that she be sent up to Robert at the castle the following nightfall.

It seems that the lovely Arlette was a girl of character. She would go, but on her own terms. All must see her. She would ride in on a fine horse, in her best clothes, accompanied by servants and in

24   *St Catherine's, Honfleur*

broad daylight. All turned out well. They were both young and attractive. But although it was a love match, Robert never married Arlette, and their son, William, born soon after, was a bastard.

Arlette lived in the castle where her son was born and most probably grew up. Before he was born, Arlette had her famous prophetic dream that from her womb there grew a tree skywards so broad that its foliage spread not only over Normandy, but also over the English kingdom as well.

The bronze statue of William the Conqueror in the Place Guillaume le Conquérant, erected in 1851, is considered to be one of the finest equestrian statues in France. Curiously enough, although practically every building in the square was bombed flat by the German *Luftwaffe* on the night of 17 August 1944, when Falaise was liberated by the Canadians, the statue was unharmed. It was as if it said, 'I, and I alone, can conquer England'.

Around its pedestal are the smaller statues of the first six dukes of Normandy, erected in 1875. Also of interest is the bronze memorial erected in 1931 in the Prix Chapel in the Talbot Tower. This bears the names of 315 prominent men who accompanied William at the Battle of Hastings in 1066. There were obviously many more, but these ones have been proved to have been there.

Falaise should be seen at night when floodlit. Every Saturday and Sunday night in June, every night in July, August, and September, pageants telling the legend of the Conqueror are held. Seats are provided for the show, and parking is free.

Lisieux

The best way to arrive at Lisieux is by train and on a summer evening when the buildings are floodlit. Then one has the ethereal and unexpected vision of its basilica on a hilltop. The contrast of a nearby skyscraper and prosaic station make it appear even more unreal, a flight of eastern fancy, a mirage rising above the treetops.

25   *Notre Dame de Grace, Honfleur*

The basilica is dedicated to Ste Thérèse and is an important centre of pilgrimage. From its grand formal garden in front there is a magnificent view over Lisieux and the surrounding country-side. Romano-Byzantine in style and with an immense rounded dome, it was started in 1923 and is still not finished. It was built to accommodate the large number of pilgrims coming to Lisieux.

Inside, it is spacious and massive, bigger than most cathedrals and ablaze with burning candles. In spite of its size, the large crypt can be jammed with people. As with Jeanne d'Arc, the worship of Ste Thérèse could be called a small industry. A shop sells candles, pictures, cards, mementoes, even on the basilica premises.

If you are interested in religion, or maybe, sociology, Lisieux is the town for you. Busloads of pilgrims come every day to visit the basilica, the Carmelite chapel and Ste Thérèse's home.

Thérèse lost her mother when she was four years old, and her father took his family of now only five daughters from Alençon to live at the house known as Les Buissonnets, on the outskirts of the then small, hilly town.

This sturdy bourgeois house, which lies up the slope of a wind-ing path, now crowded with booths selling mementoes, has been turned into a museum. Thérèse lived there for about ten years. The heavy mahogany furniture, her toys, schoolbooks and bed have all been carefully preserved.

As early as the age of nine, she decided to enter the Carmelite order, and when she was 15 she approached her father to ask his permission. This episode is now represented by a tableau of statues in the garden behind the house.

Life in a Carmelite convent at that time was very severe, especially so to someone from a comfortable home. They rose at five in the morning in summer to the clatter of castanets. All private possessions were forbidden. Inmates slept on a board across two trestles with little to lie on or cover them. A notice on the cell wall read 'My daughter why are you here?', a constant reminder of their vows. Silence was observed as much as possible. If they spoke it was to make a confession of some sin. Food was frugal. Worst of all there was the cold. Even in the coldest weather, only one room was allowed to be heated to 50°F, so it is not too surprising that the delicate, consumptive Thérèse died at such an early age.

She wrote the *Histoire d'une âme* at the instigation of her sister, Pauline, then the Mother Superior (all her sisters seemed to have taken the veil). It was written between her many duties in snatched moments, which is probably why it sometimes appears incoherent.

Ste Thérèse defined her doctrine in the *Histoire d'une âme* as the 'Little Way', the way of spiritual childhood, trust and absolute surrender to Christ. It is artless and naïve, yet at the same time heroic. She seemed to have known that it would be important after her death.

Ste Thérèse's attraction for so many people must be her ordinariness. To the more educated and sophisticated she appears sentimental and sickly sweet, but her philosophy of the 'Little Way' of obedience and humility was, I suppose, in most people's power. She bridged the gap between the metaphysical arguments of the Roman Catholic church and everyday experience.

She died in obscurity as so many other nuns have done. After a death it was customary for an obituary notice to be sent round all the other convents. It is said that the Prioress at Carmel, then a Mère de Gonzague, felt that she had not always treated Thérèse properly, and so decided to print and distribute her *Histoire* instead of the usual obituary.

This was first read in convents, where it was lent to friends, until the circle gradually widened, extending to priests and missionaries all over the world. It became very popular. Then people who were sick invoked her help and claimed that they had been cured; others swore that her spirit had appeared to them. The legend grew, especially during the First World War, when the French army adopted her as their special protectress many preferring her femininity to the soldier, Jeanne d'Arc.

Lisieux, a very old town, existing in pre-Roman times, has long been a religious city. Its bishopric, suppressed in 1802, dates back to the sixth century. Thomas à Becket took refuge there for a time.

Some relics and his vestments are to be seen in St Jacques'
church. St Peter's cathedral, twelfth to sixteenth century, which
claims to be the oldest Gothic church in Normandy, had as one of
its bishops Pierre Cauchon, who was responsible for Jeanne d'Arc's
being handed over to the English.

Because of its position on an important road junction, Lisieux
was a target for bombing in 1944, and has been rebuilt as a
modern town with much wider streets. There are not many of its
quaint old Norman houses left.

Both the basilica and St Peter's are worth visiting if you are
passing this way. You should also get a cheap meal here. Some of
the restaurant prices are very economical, ranging from nine francs
upwards and of good value. Hotels, too, are reasonable and there
are plenty of them. You should get in fairly easily, provided there
isn't a big pilgrimage taking place.

Lisieux, chief town of the Pays d'Auge, is a centre for cheeses,
such as Camembert, Pont l'Evêque and Livarot, also cider and
calvados (cider spirit). There are many pleasant drives to be had
around its lush wooded countryside, the best being to and along
its famous coast, the Côte Fleurie. That this is and was a wealthy
area can be seen by the number of châteaux and large old timbered
manor farms.

Two popular drives are to Trouville along the Toques valley,
and to Honfleur, at the start of the Côte Fleurie.

The Côte Fleurie to Caen

Honfleur has been hit not so much by bombs as by industrialization. Whichever way you enter it – car, bus or train – its
approaches are grim. However, once past the ugliness and mess
of the surroundings you round the buildings and quayside into
the Vieux Port, and the aspect changes and you are in a truly
delightful place.

Tall, narrow, rather sombre, slate-roofed houses, some half-
timbered ones dating from the sixteenth and seventeenth centuries,
cafés and restaurants, surround a harbour filled with a variety of

colourful sailing boats. The harbour was built from old fortifications and the harbourmaster's house you see at its entrance was part of the drawbridge. Behind it was the governor's house.

Honfleur, which dates from the eleventh century, like so many other Norman towns changed hands many times during the Hundred Years' War and played a fairly hectic part in the Wars of Religion. The St Leonard's quarter was badly damaged by the Protestants in 1562. Henri iv besieged Honfleur twice, once in 1590, then again in 1594.

The port and town had its heyday in the sixteenth and seventeenth centuries when trade with the American continent and East Indies made it an important maritime and commercial town. It was the home of many intrepid seafarers and explorers, the best known of them being Samuel de Champlain (1567-1635). He set sail from here in 1608 on a voyage which resulted in the foundation of Quebec. Canada, which had been claimed for France a century earlier by Jacques Cartier had been neglected until Champlain's arrival. It rapidly became a predominantly Norman colony.

Although Honfleur declined in importance as a port in the nineteenth century, when it was supplanted by Le Havre, its picturesqueness attracted writers, musicians and especially painters to settle there. Many artists gathered around the local painter, Eugène Louis Boudin at the Ferme St Siméon, about a kilometre from the town, which became a centre for the Impressionists. Monet, Sisley, Renoir, Pissarro, Cézanne all worked along this stretch of the Normandy coast.

Because of this, Honfleur now boasts a very good painting gallery, the Eugène Boudin museum, Rue Albert I°, which is devoted chiefly to those artists who painted in this area.

The Vieux Honfleur museum, just off the old port, is also worth seeing. Part of it is in the old church of St Etienne and part in old houses in the Rue de la Prison. It is quite extensive, showing rooms of old furniture, even a shop, as well as clothes, weapons, religious objects and Gallo-Roman remains.

However, no visitor to Honfleur should miss visiting the church of Ste Catherine, standing in a square opposite its tower in a most picturesque part of Honfleur. My immediate impression was of a Scandinavian stave church, because it was built out of wood, a rare phenomenon in a region so rich in good building stone.

The reason why is not known. Most likely, as it was built at the end of the Hundred Years' War, it was intended only as a temporary measure. Wood was easily obtainable, as were men who, although chiefly skilled at ship-building, could put it together and decorate it.

The result is unique. Inside are wooden pillars and walls beamed like the old manor houses in the Pays d'Auge, so that it resembles a hall rather than a church. It is spacious with two naves, while the vaulting above resembles ships' hulls turned upside down.

The bell tower, also of wood and about the same period, stands opposite the church. That it stands apart is probably due to the fact that the timbering would not withstand the weight and movement of the bells. It may also have been a safeguard against fire caused by lightning. Incidentally, the ticket for seeing the bell tower also includes a visit to the Eugène Boudin museum.

Honfleur is probably a place better to visit than to stay at for, although there are plenty of hotels and restaurants, they become very overcrowded in summer, and it has a poor beach. However, not too far away lie some of the best beaches in France.

The Côte Fleurie is a gentler coastline than that north of the Seine, and its low-lying hills sweep down almost to the sandy beaches. Behind the coast, crowded with hotels and houses, lies a pretty countryside of hedge-bound meadows, neat orchards, manor houses and stud farms.

At first, after Honfleur, is the Normandy Corniche, and a pleasant leafy road runs along hills above the sea, with a glimpse of blue through the trees. The road meets the coast again at Villenville. The corniche cliff ends at Trouville, where it is replaced by a splendid stretch of sand.

Trouville, lying at the foot of wooded hills to the north of the

Toques river, is this coast's most popular resort. It can claim two historical distinctions. One, it was the place where Henry V landed with his English army in 1417 to set out on the campaign that was to bring Normandy to the English crown. The second, and more useful, it was a favourite place of the Empress Eugénie. This is why so many of its older buildings date from the Third Empire, an architectural style which includes as many others as it can and was much liked by the newly-rich bourgeoisie.

Trouville, unlike Deauville on the opposite side of the Toques river, is geared as much to commerce as it is to holidays, and so is an all-the-year-round resort.

Deauville, internationally famous, luxurious, aristocratic, was founded by the Duc de Morny in 1866 and is built on a checkerboard plan with wide avenues. The Planches, a wooden plank promenade which runs the length of its beach (and Trouville's too), is famous for its promenade of fashionable women in smart clothes. Deauville's season starts in July and ends on the fourth Sunday in August with the Deauville Grand Prix horse race. Both Trouville and Deauville are expensive.

After Deauville, one resort comes after another, all rather alike, and overlooking vast stretches of sand. This stretch of coast, once a favourite place for the wealthy and cosmopolitan, its picturesqueness beloved by artists, is now attracting a different type of holiday-maker. Expensive hotels are being replaced by villas, rented apartments, camp sites and second homes.

The road leaves the coast after Villers-sur-Mer, renowned for its six-kilometre beach, and plunges through attractively wooded rolling countryside. At Houlgate, it returns to the sea. This is a particularly pleasant resort, combining the best of both beach and countryside.

Commercialized Dives, was where William the Conqueror set out for England. The port that he used and which was later used for shipping stone, silted up, and now only serves as an anchorage for yachts. If you visit its Gothic church, Our Lady of Dives, you will see a tablet over the door which lists names of William's chief companions.

Cabourg, facing Dives on the opposite side of the river, like Trouville became a seaside resort during the Third Empire. It is built in a fan shape, or half a cartwheel, and is leafy and green with shady avenues and villas surrounded by flowery gardens. No road runs beside the Promenade des Anglais, which borders its splendid four-kilometre beach. Fashionable and expensive, it boasts a casino and golf club.

After Franceville, the road follows the Orne estuary, first on the right side, passing Ranville, the first village in France to be liberated in June 1944, then crossing the river and canal over the Pegasus bridge to the left bank. This bridge was named after the exploit of the night 5–6 June, when it was taken by a British parachute brigade. Its possession played a vital part in the Normandy landings.

The rest of the journey to Caen is through an industrial belt even uglier than Honfleur's. This is made even worse by the fact that the previous part of the journey passed through such an attractive region.

Caen

The first Caen, which started on an island at the confluence of the rivers, Orne and Odon, became important in the eleventh century, especially when it was the favourite town of William the Conqueror.

Although not its capital, Caen is Normandy's most important city. It is progressive, well-planned, and predominantly a commercial city with some rather beautiful churches.

Caen has always played an important part in Norman history, but it was during the battle for it, lasting over two months in 1944, that it played its most dramatic and terrible rôle. Fires raged through it for 11 days, gutting its centre. Later, when the Germans retreated to new positions across the Orne, their shells added more to the debris. About two thirds of the city's buildings were totally destroyed.

The reconstruction of Caen was carried out quickly and carefully. Many narrow streets were replaced by broad thoroughfares; while those which had been attractive were restored and improved. It is a World War Two town, as its street names now show : Rue 6 Juin, Rue de la Libération, and the large flat cenotaph beside the Rue Equipes des Urgences to those shot and deported between 1940 and 1945, commemorate this dramatic episode.

Terrible though all this must have been, it has resulted in a pleasant, dignified and expanding city. Caen, with its separate residential and industrial zones, its much improved port, the creation of a new university and good communications, has attracted many major firms to settle there, thereby increasing its prosperity.

In spite of the destruction, its main sights are still the Abbaye aux Hommes and the Abbaye aux Dames.

When the ambitious William had consolidated his position as Duke of Normandy, he decided to marry his cousin, Mathilde of Flanders. However, she was less keen and stated that she would rather take the veil and enter a convent than marry a bastard. William, angered at being baulked, rode to Lille, where the Court of Flanders then was, seized Mathilde by her plaits and dragged her round the room, kicking her. Then he rode off. In spite of, or possibly because of, this rough wooing, Mathilde consented to marry him.

But they were related, and the Pope, objecting to their marriage, excommunicated them. This excommunication was later lifted in 1059 owing to the intercession of Lanfranc, William's friend and adviser. As a penance, William and Mathilde founded two abbeys at Caen, the Abbaye aux Hommes and the Abbaye aux Dames, and four hospitals.

The Abbaye aux Hommes is rather difficult to find because it is now joined up with the Town Hall and St Stephen's church. I had to walk round it before I could find a way in. There is a door near the Town Hall, but if this is closed, you should walk down the Rue Guillaume le Conquérant, past shops and houses, until you come to a square, where there is another entrance to it on the left-hand side. This integration with other buildings makes

it difficult to see properly. I think the best view of it is probably
from the Place Louis Guillouard.

Inside, the abbey is tall and cool with graceful sweeping lines,
very superior architecturally and very beautiful. Because of extensive restoration it looks quite new, but the magnificent outlines
still remain from the past. William the Conqueror's tomb before
the high altar is marked by a stone bearing his epitaph. His remains are not in the church though, as they were thrown in the
river during the Revolution.

The abbey buildings, reconstructed in the eighteenth century,
and now housing the Town Hall, can be visited during the day
(except Tuesday). There is some very fine woodwork to be seen
there.

The Abbaye aux Dames in the Place Reine Mathilde beside
a convent stands on a hill, and is some distance from Aux
Hommes.

It is easier to see as a whole, but is somewhat squat and less
attractive than Aux Hommes. This is not entirely its fault. The
spires of the church were destroyed in the Hundred Years' War
and were replaced by an ugly balustrade in the eighteenth
century.

However, the inside at first appears more vivid than Aux
Hommes. When you enter the red and blue mosaic windows have
an almost dazzling effect, lighting up the church. When you walk
towards them, then turn, the windows at the other end are of a
subdued grey, black and buff mosaic. This contrast in colours
helps to bring life to a rather dull interior.

Mathilde, like William, was buried in her church. You will see
a dark slab covered by glass behind the altar. The chapel in the
crypt, dedicated to St Nicholas, is worth seeing and is remarkably
well preserved. Incidentally, people took shelter down here during
the bombardment of the city.

Caen castle, also erected by William the Conqueror, profited in
a way from the bombing, as it now stands boldly on the hill, as it
once must have done, no longer hidden by buildings. From a
distance, it looks more imposing than it is, as it is a mere shell con-

sisting chiefly of ramparts. There are some very good views of the town from its battlements.

It boasts two museums, one of fine arts in a modern building, while the other shows the history of Normandy, and displays of pottery, clothes, kitchen utensils, etc; and also the Chapel of St George. This last is a very simply decorated memorial to those killed in action for Normandy during the centuries. There is also the tomb of an unknown victim of the bombardment in the city in 1944.

St Pierre's church, standing in a street of the same name, is near the castle and not far from the Syndicat d'Initiative. Less austere than the two abbeys, it owes its decorations to the rich merchants of Caen. The most elaborate are at the east end, built between 1518 and 1545, in Renaissance style. Behind the altar are five beautiful chapels. When you look upwards, the keystones of the first and second resemble stalactites hanging from a cave roof. St Pierre's famous fourteenth-century belfry, destroyed during the war, has been rebuilt.

Caen, because of its good position and communications, makes an excellent centre for tours and expeditions.

Near at hand is Fontaine-Henri, lying in an attractive wooded valley to the north-west. This château, built in the fifteenth and sixteenth centuries on the ruins of an old thirteenth-century fortress, is a good example of the Renaissance style. Its most unusual feature is its steeply sloping roof, set between towers and spires, which is even taller than the building below. Inside there are a remarkable François I staircase, sculptures and some interestingly furnished rooms.

Not too far away is the Swiss Normandy, the invasion beaches of the Côte Nacre and Bayeux.

Bayeux

Bayeux, capital of the Bessin country, is one of Normandy's oldest and luckiest towns.

It is old because it was the Gaullish capital of the Bajocasses,

then a Roman town, and a bishopric from the end of the fourth
century. It was captured by Rollo in 880, who married Popa,
daughter of the town's governor. Their son was William Longsword. So Bayeux could be called the cradle of the Norman
dynasty.

It was lucky because although it is only about 10 km. from the
invasion beaches it was undamaged by the war. Bayeux, first town
in France to be liberated, was taken on 7 June 1944 by the 50th
Northumbrian Division almost without a scratch.

So Bayeux remains as it was, a medieval town, its narrow streets
lined with picturesque old houses, stone bridges and all her chief
treasures intact. These – the tapestry, the cathedral and museum –
are grouped conveniently close together.

The famous Bayeux tapestry, showing William's invasion of
England, is kept in the former bishops' palace. To see it costs 4.50
francs, plus one franc for the dark green tele-translation in English. Incidentally, when you put this long receiver to your ear stand
close to the wall, otherwise the voice fades away.

The tapestry, or rather the 230-foot embroidery sewn in
coloured thread, is kept in a glass case around the walls of a
gallery. The tapestry claims to tell the whole story – from the
Norman point of view, of course – of Harold's shipwreck, his
promise to renounce the crown of England to William, his defec-
tion, and William's consequent rightful invasion of England.

The tapestry is in three sections, a top frieze, main story and
bottom frieze, and gives some interesting detail about the armour
and weapons of that period, also the people. The wicked Saxons
all have long drooping moustaches while the Normans are clean
shaven. The frieze above and below the story shows animals from
Aesop's *Fables*, or little extras about the most important events;
some are quite lewd if you know where to look.

Why it was made and who made it are not entirely certain. The
legend that it was sewn by Mathilde is now generally discounted.
Most probably it was made between 1070 and 1080 by order of
Bishop Oddo, William's turbulent half-brother, to be hung round
the nave of Bayeux Cathedral, a simple illustration to explain

what had happened and why. Some historians believe that it was made at a school of needlework in Canterbury. A very good designer would have drawn it first, then highly-skilled women did the stitching.

When you leave the tapestry, keep your ticket, for it can also be used in the museum.

The cathedral, situated between the *tapisserie* and museum, has a fascinating and highly-decorated exterior in the Norman and Gothic styles. Inside it is lofty and the nave, although not uniform, is a harmonious blend of Romanesque and Gothic. It is best to get a good general view first from the door to get the feeling of its grandeur.

Bayeux Cathedral, built by Bishop Oddo, was dedicated on 14 July 1077 to Notre Dame, and consequently to God, by the Archbishop of Rouen, Lanfranc (Archbishop of Canterbury and Primate of England), and by Thomas of Bayeaux (Archbishop of York) in the presence of William of Normandy and a large crowd of people.

There is some rather fine stained glass behind the organ, and also an ornate black pulpit, which dates from 1786. The Renaissance stalls of the choir are rather lovely.

For interest, note the side altar by the doorway, where you can see the fresco showing the murder of Thomas à Becket at Canterbury Cathedral. To see the treasure, crypt and chapter house you have to apply to the sacristy in the north transept.

The Musée Gérard, which holds exhibitions of pictures, has a small art collection (tiny pictures by Thomas Regnault and water colours and caricatures by Septime Lepipre, which are quite interesting from a historical point of view), also pottery, clothes, dolls illustrating the court of Louis XIV and collections of lace and tapestry. The museum is well set out and interesting to wander round.

Although Bayeaux is a town that grows on you – even the peals of its tinny old bells – it is better for a short visit than a long stay. Three hours are sufficient to wander through its old streets and visit the tapestry, cathedral and museum. There are not many good hotels and restaurants, and it is not a good excursion centre. There are few bus trips: even Arromanches, which is only 10 km. away, is difficult to visit by local transport. Local people just do not go there, I was told. Anyone wanting to visit the Côte Nacre invasion beaches from Bayeux will have to go by car.

The Côte Nacre and Invasion Beaches

Over recent years this coastline, lying between the Vire and Orne rivers, has become increasingly popular with holidaymakers, especially campers. Bathing is good and the beaches are wide, flat and sandy, which is why it was chosen for the allied invasion of France. Most people staying in Normandy will want to visit it, along with the famous museum at Arromanches, especially those who took part in the last war.

The landing battle is too complicated to explain properly here but, as many books have been written on it, you would get more out of your visit if you read one before you came.

Very briefly, although a landing had been envisaged by the British since 1941, it was only after the entry of the Americans into the war that it could be considered seriously. The plan, COSSAC, got the stamp of approval after the Churchill–Roosevelt meetings in Washington and Quebec in 1943, and this Calvados coast, defended by the German Seventh Army, was considered the most suitable one to attack.

Surprise, the essence of attack, was difficult to ensure. The Germans well knew that an attack would come somewhere between the Belgian coast and the mouth of the Loire, and sometime in 1944. They also knew the best time of the year and the most suitable weather conditions. All they didn't know was exactly where it would be.

Allied propaganda did its best to make the Germans think that it would probably be in the Pas de Calais area, so that they would keep their main reserves in this region.

All preparations for OVERLORD, its later official name, had to be completed by 1 June, and the invasion was to be launched on

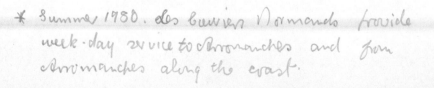

* Summer 1980. Les buviers Normands provide week-day service to Arromanches and from Arromanches along the coast.

the first suitable day thereafter, depending on a combination of meteorological factors. Eisenhower eventually chose 6 June, in spite of the uncertain weather conditions. It is interesting to note that if the invasion had not been launched on that day but had waited until the next suitable period, commencing on the 19th, it would have bumped into the worst storm in living memory.

At dawn on D-day, 6 June 1944, the British and Commonwealth ground forces established beach heads at areas known by the code names Sword, Juno and Gold, linking up with the airborne troops dropped to the east of Pegasus bridge. They obtained the critical foothold ashore with fewer casualties than expected. The Americans landing on the beaches with code names Omaha and Utah only linked up with their airborne troops' flank after the capture of Carentan on 12 June, and experienced more difficulty.

Intensive Allied air action prevented the German air force from interfering with the landings. Differences between the German commanders, von Rundstedt and Rommel, on the conduct of the campaign, also helped. Rommel won, but he had insufficient inland defences. Once his Atlantic wall was broken he could not collect enough troops together to endanger the bridgehead on the beach, and Allied bombing prevented reinforcements. Also the Germans, still believing that the main invasion was yet to come in the Pas de Calais, kept a large force there. The British and Canadians pressed on towards Caen, the hinge of the front. US troops in the Cotentin peninsula worked down towards them.

The Arromanches museum is the main place to visit along the invasion beaches and is quite fascinating. Here you can see a Royal Navy film of the actual landings, listen to a talk using lit-up models, a sort of *son et lumière*, and look at the collection of war paraphernalia, equipment and flags, etc., all well-labelled.

In the sea outside is the Mulberry Harbour which was towed across the Channel in 1944 to be used by the British troops, and which was in service up to the end of August 1944, when Cherbourg and Antwerp became partially available.

Probably the best place to start a drive along the invasion beaches is from Caen (bus companies also do a tour), perhaps making a diversion to Bayeux and finishing at Carentan, in the Cotentin.

From here, if you wish, you can drive to Barfleur, via the Utah beach, making a detour to the Saire valley, then drive across the Cotentin to Fermanville and take the picturesque corniche road to Cherbourg.

12. Manche

Manche is the French for 'channel' and this department takes its name from this stretch of sea. Manche's 200 miles of fine sandy beaches, especially those between Carteret and Mont St Michel, are becoming increasingly popular with holidaymakers, particularly campers.

Inland it is a department of small hills, cut by short streams, a region of apple orchards or pastures for cattle and horses. The Manche has the largest cattle population of any other: it even exceeds the human one. Cooperative processing and marketing is highly developed here, and the production of butter, cheese and milk powder are its chief industries.

It is a region of scattered farmsteads and hamlets, rather than villages, but there are many small market towns. The people, once very poor, developed many small industries, such as weaving and copperware, some of which still survive.

The Manche is made up of the Normandy Bocage, which has a landscape of woodlands and small meadows, bounded by tall hedges, and the Cotentin peninsula, which is more varied.

The Cotentin Peninsula

The Cotentin's rocky coastline is similar to that of Brittany and Cornwall. The peninsula is divided from the Bocage by low-lying marshland, grazed over by cattle, and from which peat is gathered. If the sea here rose by more than ten metres the Cotentin would again become the island it once was.

During the eleventh and twelfth centuries the Cotentin was the home of those Normans, such as the Hauteville brothers, who distinguished themselves by founding kingdoms in Sicily and southern Italy. Their armies were an outlet for the peninsula's teeming poverty-stricken population. This rough country has often played a part in wars and uprisings: the last one was in OVERLORD, when American troops landed either side of the Vire river to establish the Omaha and Utah beachheads. Their objective was to cut the Cotentin in two and seize Cherbourg, a much more formidable task than they had realised in this wooded, hedged country.

Cherbourg, lying at the mouth of the Divette river, overlooked by the steep Montagne du Roule, is both a naval base and an important transatlantic and ferry passenger port.

Spacious, sprawling and new, this city by the sea is chiefly a place to pass through. Its main function for holidaymakers being a point of departure for home, the coastal regions, or a journey through France, especially for those with cars. Cherbourg is not so good for the humble pedestrian, who will have to walk quite a distance from the railway station to the Gare Maritime, which, when boats are not in, resembles a stranded dead city, lying amidst quays, sheds and boats, only a distant cousin of the town behind.

Although Cherbourg was used as a port by Bronze Age traders, was a Roman station, and played quite an important part in the Hundred Years' War, it was developed later than other ports of similar size. This is because it was surrounded on three sides by rocks but the fourth side, the north one, was exposed to the sea, and installations set up there soon washed away. The large breakwater there now was started during the time of Louis XVI, continued by Napoleon, but not finally completed until the Napoleon III era.

The Germans did as much damage to the harbour as they could before they evacuated Cherbourg in June 1944. But the Americans were so badly in need of a port – their own Mulberry Harbour had been wrecked during storms – that they managed to get it into order again by October, when it became the main port for supplies during the Ardennes offensive. The underwater pipeline, PLUTO, laid between the Isle of Wight and Cherbourg, supplied the Allies with petrol from 12 August 1944.

Many people are likely to find themselves in Cherbourg, probably with a few hours of waiting to fill. The town is quite pleasant, with some good food shops. The best place to make for fairly near at hand is the promenade to the left of the port. Here is a small garden, brooded over by a statue of Napoleon, overlooking a good sandy beach.

If you've more time to spare you can drive up to the Roule Fort, which was the chief pocket of German resistance in 1944. From the terrace there is a good view of the town and harbour. Here also is the War and Liberation museum, which uses maps to tell the story of the Allied landings in June 1944 through to the final German surrender in May 1945.

A nearby château worth visiting is the attractively situated sixteenth-century one at Nacqueville, about 9 km. from Cherbourg (N13 and D45), but not on Tuesdays. Or, only 5 km. away is the picturesque park, combining tropical plants and beech trees, surrounding Tourlaville château (N801, D63).

To the east of Cherbourg lie the lovely wooded Val de Saire (approximately a three-hour trip), a name which applies to the whole of this northeast peninsula, and the two small harbour resorts, Barfleur and St Vaast.

Barfleur, best seen at high tide, has a picturesque port now filled with pleasure craft. The view from the west end of its rugged old church towards the Gateville lighthouse is magnificent. This lighthouse, the tallest in France, is open to visitors. From its top there is a splendid panorama over the east coast of the Cotentin peninsula and the Saire river disappearing down into the sea. Although the sea here is shallow there are swift currents and it can be very rough. In fact, if it were not for the jetty to the north of the town, Barfleur would be swamped. Many ships have foundered, especially on the rocks on which the Gateville lighthouse now stands. The most famous of these was the *Blanche Nef*, which was carrying William, only legitimate son of Henry I and heir to the English throne, to England in 1120. That this should have happened was also due to the intoxication of the pilot and crew. The prince might have escaped in a small boat had he not insisted on its turning back to rescue his natural sister, the Countess of Mortagne. On arriving back at the sinking ship, his boat was at once filled with a crowd of despairing wretches and they all sank together.

Small but busy St Vaast-la-Hougue is of even greater interest to English visitors. It was here that Edward III's army landed, an expedition that was to end in the French defeat at Crécy. Later landings here were those of Henry IV and Henry V. More important still, it was near here in 1692 that a combined English and Dutch fleet frustrated the attempt of James II to regain his English crown. They destroyed the French fleet, which intended to engage the English one, while an army of French and Irish troops which had gathered at La Hougue landed in England.

The fortifications you see there now were erected as a result of this engagement – rather like locking the stable door once the horse has gone. St Vaast today is first important as an oyster-breeding centre then as a resort, as it has a good bathing beach and fine sheet of water for sailing.

On the other side of Cherbourg (N12, D45) lies the bleak granite spine, La Hague, which although flat has a sort of wild grandeur. There are no trees to withstand the gales, but the short turf is criss-crossed with stone walls to protect the sheep and divide it into enclosures. On an island of low rocks stands a tall lighthouse to warn shipping.

The Nez de Joubourg, a long rugged promontory encircled by reefs, is one of the most spectacular sights of the coast, especially when seen from the Nez de Voidries (approached from Goury, D401, then D202 from Dammery).

From Beaumont (N801 from Dammery) to the seaside resort Barneville-Carteret, is a picturesque drive. Although the road does not hug the coast, the countryside is fairly low-lying and there are good views of the sea and Channel Islands beyond.

The inland wooded country turns to plains, rather like a vast open park, where brindled cows and horses graze, especially around Ste Mère Eglise, Normandy's chief cattle market town.

The Bocage

Although Cherbourg is the largest town in the Manche, Saint-Lô is the departmental capital.

One's first sight of it is of its *Enclos,* the vast wall, partly rock, partly built, of the old town, with the tops of the houses and church peeping just above.

Known as Briovera in Roman times, it owes its present name to Landus, Bishop of Coutances, who died in 565. It was an important fortress town and also a centre of the weaving industry during the Middle Ages. In 1574 it embraced Calvinism, and was subsequently stormed by the Catholics. In 1796, Saint-Lô replaced Coutances as capital of the department. Alas, though, as a key-point of German resistance in the Second World War, it suffered such tremendous damage that earned itself the name, 'Capital of the Ruins'.

The construction of the new town began in 1948. In a way you could say that the bombing did some good in that it revealed and clarified the outline of its old ramparts. As with the castle at Caen, they are only a shell, but here they do enclose a small town, if a rebuilt one, behind them.

Numerous paths lead up this grand aspect of rocks, half-covered in foliage, into the new 'old' town. Wherever you come out, it is not likely to be far from the fourteenth- to fifteenth-century Notre Dame church, still undergoing repairs, and the symbol of the town that was. The extent of the damage done to it is shown by the photo in the church taken of its roofless nave, with the sturdy crucifix hanging dramatically above the rubble. Another picture on the wall shows the bombed houses surrounding the church.

The cenotaph in the Place Général de Gaulle, a half-ruined porch covered in leaves and dedicated to the victims of Nazi aggression, makes a strong contrast to the tall modernistic pillar, topped by a lion nearby. The walk round the Promenade des Ramparts, which begins near here, gives a good view of the town below the rocks. New houses, blocks of flats and the thin Vire river appear neat and well-planned, as is all the countryside around.

Saint-Lô, lying on main roads, makes a good centre for excursions. Nearby is the Vire valley, a quite pleasant 40 km. tour, during which you can visit the rebuilt Matignon castle, which possesses some interesting old tapestries and furniture, and also the magnificent Ham rocks.

To the west of Saint-Lô is the country town of Coutances, standing on a hill and crowned by one of the loveliest cathedrals in France.

Coutances, known as Cosedic by the Celts, had its name changed to Constantia by the Romans in honour of their Emperor. Coutances suffered badly during the Norman invasions, but later became one of their favourite towns. In 1066 one of its bishops, Geoffrey de Montbray, and several nobles from round about accompanied William on his Conquest of England. Geoffrey also started on the construction of the first part of the cathedral, the nave, while the sons Tancarville helped get the rest of it finished. However, after the destruction of the town by fire in 1218 a new cathedral, Gothic in style, was erected on the old Romanesque one, a difficult task involving considerable technical skill.

Most fortunately, Coutances Cathedral was spared by the bombing and only lost the spire above the central tower. As it stands at the highest point in the town and faces a large square, the Place du Parvis, rebuilt after the war, it is possible to get a good view of its twin west towers and the façade between.

Inside, you stand at the beginning of the nave to get a good general view of its beautiful upswept lines. There is little ornamentation to distract. The large lantern tower above the transept crossing is a masterpiece of construction, and the best example of its type in Normandy.

Coutances also boasts a very fine garden, once belonging to a private house. Terraces and steps descend the slopes, while trees form a leafy background to its lawns and flowerbeds. In summer this and the cathdral are floodlit and a *son et lumière* performance is held on Thursday, Saturday, Sunday and holidays.

The plain but majestic ruins of the Abbey of Hambye lie to the south east of Coutances. A guided tour round its church and buildings takes about an hour. It is closed on Tuesdays.

Granville, a somewhat grim but quaint town, situated on the coast at the mouth of the river Bisque, is in two parts; one is a fortified seaport, the other a bathing resort.

Its old town, the Haute Ville, built on a promontory, has a sort of austere attraction. Straight roads lead up between eighteenth-century houses to its robust granite Notre Dame. From the Place de l'Istre, an enormous square, you can see as far as Brittany on a clear day.

Granville should be of interest to the English as it was they who founded the town in 1439. Unable to capture Mont St Michel in the south, they decided to consolidate their position in this part of Normandy by building a strong defence on this rocky promontory stretching out to sea. Unfortunately the French captured it before it was finished, and found it very useful indeed themselves, as did the Germans in World War Two, when they converted it into a formidable strongpoint.

The new town, which grew round it below is popular in spite of its small beach, boasts a casino and golf course and is a centre for yachtsmen. From the harbour there are daily trips to the Islands of Chausey and the Channel Islands.

Avranches, standing on a hill above the Sées estuary, is most attractively situated. Moreover, it has the honour of having been the see of the Bishop St Aubert, who founded Mont St Michel Abbey across the bay. One night, the story goes, St Aubert had a strange dream in which the ghost of St Michael, the Archangel, appeared and commanded him to build an oratory on top of the mount.

Avranches was a bishops' see from 511 to 1790, when its cathdral seems to have collapsed, never alas to be rebuilt. But you can still see the paving stone, which was once in the cathedral, where Henry II kneeled to do public penance for the murder of Thomas à Becket.

Avranches also has the honour of being the place where on 1 August 1944, General Patton launched his famous counter-attack. His army smashed through the German lines, part going towards Brittany, and part towards Le Mans. A monument now marks the place where Patton stood before the start of this offensive. The square surrounding it, planted with trees from the U.S., is now regarded as American territory.

People interested in old manuscripts might like to see some in the Avranchin museum dating from the eighth to the fifteenth centuries, which have come from Mont St Michel Abbey. Those more interested in the bizarre might care to see St Aubert's skull in the St Gervais and St Protais Basilica. The dent in it is supposed to have been made by the imperious Archangel Michael when St Aubert at first ignored his instructions to build an oratory on the rock.

One of the main sights of Avranches is its botanical gardens, filled with exotic plants, once belonging to the former bishop's palace. From its terrace is a magnificent view across the bay of that strange conical shape, Mont St Michel, which looks at its most romantic by moonlight.

This town and abbey, ringed by ramparts, built on a rock, rising abruptly from a great stretch of treacherous silver sand, is the wonder of Normandy, and of France, too.

Centuries ago, the whole of the bay in which it stands was a vast forest, extending as far as the Channel Islands. Two rocky summits towered above this mass of trees. The one on which St Michel now stands was used first as a place of worship by the Druids and dedicated to the sun. This was later replaced by a Roman temple to Jove. Eventually, Christian hermits took possession of the rocks and built chapels on both of them.

Then came the great tides of the early eighth century, which cut the Channel Islands off from the mainland, turning the rocks into islands. These became places of refuge for people flying from the pillaging, burning Vikings. A little town grew round the monks' colony on St Michel's mount.

After St Aubert had built his oratory there it became so important a place of pilgrimage that in 966, Richard Duke of Normandy had the oratory replaced by a Benedictine abbey.

It grew rich, receiving generous endowments from Normandy, Brittany and England – the priory of St Michael's Mount in Cornwall was given to Mont St Michel by Edward the Confessor – and it became a celebrated place of learning. When it was burned down in 1203, the French king, Philippe Auguste, compensated the monks by providing for the construction of La Merveille, the superb Gothic structure that can be seen there today.

La Merveille had varying fortunes, being used as a fortress as well as an abbey during the Hundred Years' War. Its greatest period was during the time of Louis XIV when it was enlarged and made more beautiful. But its decline had already set in before the French Revolution, when the monks were obliged to leave. For a brief period, it was known as the Mount of Liberty. In 1811 Napoleon had it made into a prison, which it remained until 1863. It was not until 1966, its millenary year, that Benedictine monks held services in the great church again.

The first time, I saw Mont St Michel was on a wet day, when its abbey and church poked out of the misty rain like an enchanted castle. As its island was then almost surrounded by sea, I had to cross to the town below from the shore by a long strip of land, a natural drawbridge.

Buildings climbed the steep rock in terraces above high walls up to St Michel, glittering with wet, a shining tribute to the skill and love of those long ago monks. Each granite block, brought from Brittany or the Chausey Islands, had had to be hauled up to the site, no mean feat for that period.

The name Merveille really refers to the superb Gothic fortress abbey on the north side of the mount, the buildings of which are fit for kings, and indeed many were entertained here. The cloisters are particularly beautiful and should not be missed.

I felt like a real medieval pilgrim as I passed through the old archway, then up a steep slope past shops stacked with souvenirs, for this quaint old town now exists entirely on tourists and pilgrims. It was a long trek before I finally arrived at the twisting stone stairway of 90 steps leading up to the church.

There was a wonderful view of the surrounding flat land from the terrace outside, making the hard climb worthwhile. On one side, where the river runs into the sea, is the boundary line of the province, putting Mont St Michel just in Normandy. On the other side is Brittany.

APPENDIX

How to Get to Brittany and Normandy

1. *BRITTANY*
   Sea/rail, without a car
   Up to now, Brittany has been quite difficult to get to without a car because of its lack of large passenger ports, while the ports such as Cherbourg and Le Havre, in Normandy, do not link up easily by rail with resorts in Brittany. St Malo can only be reached from England by changing at the Channel Islands. However, now that the Plymouth/Roscoff line has opened. this should make things easier, especially for people holidaying in the west of Brittany.
   Sea/rail with a car
   Southampton – Cherbourg
   Southampton – Le Havre
   Weymouth – St Malo, via Channel Islands
   Plymouth – Roscoff
   Air
   Heathrow, London – Dinard, La Baule, Nantes, Quimper,
   Rennes
   Plymouth – Morlaix

2. *NORMANDY*
   Sea/rail, with or without a car
   Newhaven – Dieppe
   Southampton – Le Havre

Southampton – Cherbourg
Weymouth – Cherbourg

Air

Heathrow, London – Deauville,
Gatwick, London – Le Havre,
Gatwick, London – Rouen

TRANSPORT

You really need a car in Normandy and Brittany, unless you have a lot of time and patience. Normandy is better linked by train than Brittany, where the service is probably about the worst in France. Buses in both provinces can be fun to travel on, and they are certainly a very relaxed way of getting around: also you do meet ordinary people. Bus timetables are displayed at the Gare Routiére, which is usually close to the railway station. Sometimes you have to buy your ticket beforehand, perhaps in a café near the stop (*Auto Arrêt*). Stopping places are not always very well-marked, so it is a good idea to check the exact place and time of the bus with local people. Bus times are casual, probably due to the fact that so many of the drivers act as 'postmen', delivering parcels as well as people at stops. On the other hand trains are very punctual.

ACCOMMODATION

Hotel prices are very variable in France, depending on where they are and who uses them. Those used by tourists are usually the most expensive. Charges are lower away from big highways. Before booking at a hotel, ascertain what the price will be (you can check this with the price which should be written up in the room itself). If *'service compris'*, the tip will be included in the price, otherwise there might be a supplement of $12\frac{1}{2}$ to 15% on the bill. Most hotel rooms in Normandy and Brittany are clean and have comfortable beds. Some seem to economize on lighting arrangements. Also on soap! — very few hotels provide soap. French plumbing sometimes make strange noises. At one hotel I stayed in, I spent about half an hour searching my room for a cat (although I couldn't imagine how it got in), until I realised that the mews were caused by pipes. Bolsters are sometimes kept in the wardrobe.

PLACES TO STAY AT

The Syndicat d'Initiative (which you should always call at when visiting a new place in order to get maps and information) will give a list of recommended hotels and restaurants. They will phone up and book for you if you wish (you will be charged for the call). Their offices usually close about 6.30 p.m. If you are booking on your own during the season (July/August) or during a weekend in summer, you shouldn't leave looking for accommodation much after six. If you are planning to make a long stay in one place, write and ask the local Syndicat d'Initiative to send you a list of recommended hotels.

You can rent a villa or flat in Normandy and Brittany. Make enquiries about this at the French Tourist Office, 178 Piccadilly, London W.1., or write to the Syndicat d'Initiative of the area of your choice (address can be had from the French Tourist Office).

Camping is one of the cheapest ways of holidaying in Normandy and Brittany, where there are some splendid camp sites. There are four categories, which are graded according to the facilities provided. You do not have to book in advance (except for some of the de luxe sites). You just drive in, as for a hotel, and ask if there is space for you. The International Membership card of the Camping Club of Great Britain entitles you to stay at any of the official camp sites throughout France. It is often possible to hire tents if you don't want to travel with heavy gear. A useful address is The Touring Club of France, 178 Piccadilly, London W.1. for further information about this. Michelin produces a guide : 'Camping and Caravanning in France'. There is also the FFCC Guide Official Camping Caravanning.

RESTAURANTS

As with hotels it pays to shop around as prices are very variable. Menu prices are pinned up on restaurant doors. *'Service compris'* means tip and service included, otherwise there will be approximately 12% extra on the bill. Bread is always provided free at meals, and water too (ask for a *carafe d'eau*). Sometimes wine is, but this doesn't often happen, and the wine would probably be rather a rough one. Railway stations often supply good, reasonably-priced meals. You are unlikely to get a proper meal anywhere under a £1 in France. But a meal at about £1.50 is a great deal better value than its counterpart in England would be.

SHOPPING
In my view the small shop, usually run by Madame and family, is cheaper than the large supermarkets. Markets are better value still. You can find out when and where they are held at the local Syndicat d'Initiative.

GASTRONOMY

NORMANDY
Rich cream predominates in Norman cooking. Most famous cheeses are, Pont l'Evêque, Livarot, Camembert (Auge region is best), Suisses and Demi Sel from Bray.

Rouen is famous for its duck (especially pâtés) and sugar apples; Caen for tripe and caramels; Ferté Macé for tripe; Mont St Michel for omelettes; Dieppe for sole; Vire for chitterling; Avranches for white pudding; Honfleur for shrimps and cockles; Villenville for mussels; St Vaast for oysters; La Hague for lobsters.

Normandy, a great cattle country, is also renowned for its meat, especially Cotentin lamb.

Cider is drunk everywhere and with most foods. The Auge Valley cider is reckoned the best. Calvados (which takes 12 to 15 years to mature) a cider spirit, is drunk in the middle of a meal – the '*Trou* (hole) *Normand*' – and also at the end with black coffee. There is also Poiré (perry alcohol), and Bénédictine (produced at Fécamp).

BRITTANY
Brittany, surrounded by water, is a paradise for fish-eaters, especi-

ally those of shellfish – crabs, lobsters, oysters, cockles, mussels, etc. Lobster Armorocaine, which is lobster served grilled with cream and a special sauce, is one of Brittany's most famous dishes. Salmon and trout are popular dishes in the Black Mountain and Monts d'Arrée area. Highly-flavoured mutton from sheep pastured in the Prés Salés, salty fields round Mont St Michel, is another favourite. Crêpes (pancakes) – savoury or sweet – are served with ham, cheese and jam, also cider. There are many crêperies in Brittany. Vegetables and fruit are plentiful – I have never eaten better tomatoes and apples than in Brittany. Nantes is famous for cakes, biscuits and sweets.

The best cider comes from the Fouesnant area, but it is not as good as that produced in Normandy. Brittany only produces wine in the Rhuys peninsula, and it is of poor quality. Muscadet, grown round Nantes, is the standard drink. Popular wines drunk in Brittany are Gros Plant and Côtes de Layon, which both come from the Loire region and go well with shellfish.

UNUSUAL HOLIDAYS IN BRITTANY AND NORMANDY
Sleep in a castle :
    Write to the French Tourist Office in London to enquire about staying in château - hotels.

Attend a Bagpipe Festival in Brest in August :
    Write to the Syndicat d'Initiative de Brest,
    Pavillon du Tourisme, Place la Liberté, Brest.

Go on a golfing holiday :
    Write to Fédération Française de Golf, 11 Rue de Bassane, 75 Paris 16.

A lorry drivers' holiday :
    You can eat and sleep cheaply at a Relais des Routiers. Get addresses of Les Routiers from Hachette (Booksellers), 4 Regent Place, London W1.

Ride a horse in Normandy:
   Write to the Association de Tourisme Equestre, 60 Grande Rue,
   61 Alençon.

Go on a caravan holiday in Normandy or Brittany :
   Write to Cheval Voyages, 4 Rue de l'Echelle, 75 Paris 1.

A cooking course at Dieppe :
   Write to Syndicat d'Initiative, Boulevard Général de Gaulle,
   76 Dieppe.

Attend a French summer school:
   Write to Cours Universitaire d'Eté, Faculté des Lettres,
   35 Rennes-Ville Jean.

For information about Son et Lumière and Pardons, apply to the
French Tourist Office in London, who have special lists printed.

BOOKS ABOUT BRITTANY AND NORMANDY

BRITTANY
NOVELS
Balzac, *Les Chouans*
Victor Hugo, *Quatre Vingt Treize*
Pierre Loti, *Pêcheur d'Islande (An Iceland Fisherman)*
Julien Gracq, *Un Beau Ténébreux (The Dark Stranger)*

NON-FICTION
Peter Anson, *Mariners of Brittany,* Dent, 1931
Anatole Le Braz, *The Land of Pardons,* Methuen, 1906
Glyn Daniel, *The Hungry Archaeologist in France,* Faber & Faber, 1963
Glyn Daniel, *Megaliths in History,* Faber & Faber, 1973
Henry Myhill, *Brittany,* Faber & Faber, 1969
Nora K. Chadwicke, *Early Brittany,* University of Wales Press, 1969

NORMANDY
Sir Frank Stenton, *The Bayeux Tapestry,* Phaidon Press, 1957
David C. Douglas, *William The Conqueror,* Eyre & Spottiswoode, 1964
Charles Homer Haskins, *Normans in European History,* Constable, 1914
Viscount Montgomery, *Normandy to the Baltic,* Hutchinson, 1946
Dwight D. Eisenhower, *Crusade in Europe,* Heinemann, 1948
Mrs Robert Henrey, *Madeleine, Young Wife,* Dent, 1960
Anthony Glyn, *The Seine,* Weidenfeld & Nicolson, 1966
William Gaunt, *The Impressionists,* Thames & Hudson, 1970

Index